MAKE UP YOUR MIND

HEAVEN OR HELL

GOD TOLD ME TO TELL YOU...

WRITTEN BY JOSEPHINE ELLIS

Dedication

This book is dedicated to my Father GOD, his son JESUS, my parents JW and CLEORA ADAMS. To JOHNNIE ELLIS and my children CORVETTE, JASMINE, JOHNATHAN, JOSEPHINE, and grandchildren. To the ADAMS and ELLIS family. To everyone who is waiting for Jesus's return to earth.

MAKE UP YOUR MIND HEAVEN OR HELL

GOD TOLD ME TO TELL YOU...

ISBN: 978-1-7338169-7-7

LCCN: 2019903239

TABLE OF CONTENTS

INTRODUCTION

There are only two commandments God gave us to follow, love God first, and love others second. Love is the fulfillment of God's laws. Investing in love is the greatest investment in your lifetime on this earth.

You were created to worship God in love and truth. God loves you so much he sent his only son Jesus to die for your sins. Whoever believes in Jesus would have eternal life. **(1st John 5:11) "And this is the record, God hath given to us eternal life, and this life is in his son."** You were brought back to God with the price of Jesus Christ's death. If you confessed Jesus is the son of God, he is your savior who has redeemed you from Satan (the devil) and eternal life in hell.

Your life doesn't belong to you anymore when you became a child of God. Jesus has provided your salvation; his death gave you immortality; sickness, death, and poverty have no authority in your life. He introduced eternity in heaven on earth, the Holy Ghost Spirit, gospel of grace, faith in him, and to remove all demonic spirits in your life.

Jesus will come back one day to make a new heaven on earth. No one can predict when he will return to claim his kingdom; live your life like he is coming every day. **(Matthew 24: 42, 50) "Watch therefore: for ye know not what hour your Lord doth come. The lord of that servant shall come in a day when he look not for him, and in an hour that he is not aware of."** Start preparing for Jesus's return, you never know when he will return to claim his kingdom. Jesus promises you a new heaven and earth in this world when he returns**. (Revelation 21:1) "And I saw a new heaven and a new earth: for the first heaven and the first earth were passed away; and there was no more sea."**

Jesus positioned you to receive grace from God who loves you unconditionally. The devil is your enemy he is a self-destructor, he wants you to join him in hell, and he has no authority, unless you give him your authority.

Miracles and power are in your own tongue, you have to speak God's words over your entire life. Meditate on God's promises not your problems, and only use God's words when praying and speaking. **(Psalms 115:16) "The heaven, even the heavens, are the LORD'S: but the earth hath he given to the children of men."** Heaven is God's home, but this world was given to people. This world belongs to you, stop acting like you are a renter.

(Genesis 1:27-28) "So God created man in his own image, in the image of God created he him; male and female created he them. And God blessed them, and God said unto them, be

fruitful, and multiply, and replenish the earth, and subdue it: and have dominion over the fish of the sea, and over the fowl of the air, and over every living thing that moved upon the earth." Take back what the devil has stolen, by using Jesus's power of authority he gave you to cast out the devil and his demons in your life. **(Luke 10:19) "Behold, I give unto you power to tread on serpents and scorpions, and over all the power of the enemy: and nothing shall by any means hurt you."** God has defeated the devil when he gave your spirit immortality. Be watchful, draw near to God, because the world today is transforming national laws to introduce an antichrist world making hell on earth.

Chapter One

GOD LOVE

It is time for you to make up your mind, do you want to go to heaven or hell. Jesus's kingdom on earth will happen rapidly. The day the Lord returns will be an astonishing day, and he will reward everyone according to their faith and love, he will make a new heaven in this world. God is Alpha and Omega, he is the first and the last. Blessed are the people who keep his commandments (to love), they will have the right to the kingdom and eternal life in heaven on earth. **(Revelation 22:12-14) "And, behold, I come quickly; and my reward is with me, to give every man according as his work shall be. I am Alpha and Omega, the beginning and the end, the first and the last. Blessed are they that do his commandments, that they may have right to the tree of life, and may enter in through the gates into the city."**

God created heaven and earth and whosoever thinks different is in denial! If you are going to believe in something in this world, why not believe there is a God? He has given you immortality, he is willing to love you unconditionally. Who is not willing to accept the gifts of immortality and to be loved unconditionally?

This power would have only come from a source of a spirit of holiness and love. God gave you dominion over the entire earth;

everything in it and around the world belongs to you. This is your inheritance from the beginning of this world. Look at what God gave you, he trusted you with this whole world. He never intended for you to know evil, only his love and to love others.

God made you in his image, you were built to live for eternity; your spirit is biologically made for immortality, your soul (the heart) was made to love everyone. The human body is made of three parts—a spirit, soul, and body. The spirit is powerful, supernatural, and in direct contact with God and the Holy Ghost Spirit. Your soul is the character of your heart, mind, and your body is made of human organ systems. You are made wonderfully, marvelous and fearless perfect in God eyes.

God loved you the moment he breathed into your nostrils, giving you the power of eternal life. The devil tricked Adam and Eve, God's first human creations lost their freedom to maintain immortality on earth. They brought sins and sorrow into the earth allowing Satan (the devil) to steal their position with God. Satan wants the power of your worship, Satan wants you to hate. God gave you his spirit to love and worship him only. The devil is a liar, the father of lies, the truth is not in him, neither is love.

(Genesis 3:1, 3) "Now the serpent was more subtle than any beast of the field which the LORD God had made. And he said unto the woman, Yea, hath God said, ye shall not eat of

every tree of the garden? But of the fruit of the tree which is in the midst of the garden, God hath said, ye shall not eat of it, neither shall ye touch it, lest ye die."

Let me speak clearly, there is a devil that hates you because God loves you, he is your enemy, don't believe his lies. **(Genesis 3:4, 6) "And the serpent said unto the woman, ye shall not surely die. And when the woman saw that the tree *was* good for food, and that it *was* pleasant to the eyes, and a tree to be desired to make *one* wise, she took of the fruit thereof, and did eat, and gave also unto her husband with her; and he did eat."** The devil told Adam and Eve they wouldn't die. Do not fall for the oldest trick in this world, the devil is still using today to make you believe God did not tell you sin causes death in your physical body, and to love him with all of your heart, mind, soul, and to love everyone.

After Adam and Eve were disobedient, God knew he had to feed them with a long-handled spoon. He would have to show them his way to live life with the knowledge of good and evil, and how to love unconditionally. Adam and Eve's rebellion is the source of sins, sickness, poverty, and physical death in this world. They lost their ability to live a spiritual life on earth for eternity. God made it perfectly clear if they eat from the tree of life they would physically die. Adam and Eve's failure caused the human race to lose out on a supernatural life on earth. They made everyone on earth responsible for working out their own salvation. God had limited his blessing to provide for everyone.

(Genesis 3:22-23) "And the LORD God said, Behold, the man is become as one of us, to know good and evil: and now, lest he put forth his hand, and take also of the tree of life, and eat, and live forever. Therefore, the LORD God sent him forth from the Garden of Eden, to till the ground from whence he was taken." God had already prepared a way for the human race to return back into his character to love, and to have eternal life; by offering blood sacrifice, laws, something or someone has to die. His plan was to enter into this world and die for you to love him freely. Love will give you the lifestyle of heaven on earth, it makes the presence of God noticeable in your life.

GOD COVENANT

God knew that the sacrificing of animals, and the Ten Commandments would not be sufficient to cover the sins in the world. This is where he showed the whole world how he loves. He put his spirit in a human body, Jesus was God in the flesh. **(Hebrew 10:8, 10, 16-17) "Above when he said, Sacrifice and offering and burnt offerings and offering for sin thou would not, neither had pleasure therein; which are; offered by the law. By which we are sanctified through the offering of the body of Jesus Christ once for all. This *is* the covenant that I will make with them after those days, saith the Lord, I will put my laws into their hearts, and in their minds will I write them; And their sins and iniquities will I remember no more."**

God took Jesus's life to save your life, this world was in bondage held up for ransom by the devil, because of disobedience (sins). **(Roman 5:8) "But God commendeth his love toward us, in that, while we were yet sinners, Christ died for us."** He offered his body has a living blood sacrifice for the world's sins. Jesus's death paid the price, for your salvation and freedom from enteral punishment.

Your life does not belong to you, Jesus paid hell in full so you can serve God only. This is why you are living in this world today to worship God. God is looking upon the earth, he sees that the world has lost the way again, becoming lovers of ourselves and making decisions without consulting him first.

You were given grace, and freedom at the cost of Jesus's life to live your life loving God and others. Heaven is above the earth, and God's standards are above this world, he wants you to love him and take on his character over the world's ways. **(Isaiah 55:9) "For as the heavens are higher than the earth, so are my ways higher than your ways, and my thoughts than your thoughts."**

God wanted a family that loved him, so he blessed this world through one man, Abraham. He made a promise to bless Abraham and his seed, through God's promise, everyone is blessed. **(Genesis 12: 1, 3) "Now the LORD had said unto Abram, Get thee out of thy country, and from thy kindred, and from thy father's house, unto a land that I will shew thee. And I will bless them that bless thee, and curse him that cursed thee: and in thee shall all families of the earth be blessed."** God wants you to call on him for directions to the promises and his assignment in your life. You are the seed of Abraham; the blessing of the covenant is on your life. Abraham was a rich man and all of his wealth belongs to you, this is your inheritance from

God. Have faith in God, consult with him daily concerning your life, so he can reveal his path and purpose for your life.

God prepared a plan for your life, seek his purpose in your life, he will guide you if you ask him. Begin to seek God by worshiping, praising, and giving him all the glory that is due to him. He had to sacrifice his son Jesus's life so that you can be free to love him not this world.

You will be responsible to praise and worship God daily when heaven comes on earth. Always thank God for his son who has given everyone redemption with the gospel of grace. Have faith in Jesus he has canceled out your works to inherit heaven.

(Colossians 1:5, 12, 13) "For the hope which is laid up for you in heaven, whereof ye heard before in the word of the truth of the gospel. Giving thanks unto the Father, which hath made us meet to be partakers of the inheritance of the saints in light: Who hath delivered us from the power of darkness, and hath translated us into the kingdom of his dear Son." Through the blood of Jesus, he has given you eternal life, he has absolved your mind from unqualified labor to serve God. Jesus has offered you reconciliation back to God by his death. **(Hebrew 9:14) "How much more shall the blood of Christ, who through the eternal Spirit offered himself without spot to God, purge your conscience from dead works to serve the**

living God?" Your health and wealth come from God. If it had not been for God being on your side, your enemies would have destroyed you. Have faith in God who gave you grace and mercy when he decided to love you unconditionally. God's DNA is love. If you lack love, you only need to get a blood transfusion and accept Jesus Christ's blood. The blood of Jesus cleansed, and saved you from the rapture of God; allowing you to be seated and accepted into heaven.

GOD WORDS

The words of God are your weapon, piercing to divide the soul and spirit. His words will make you look at your heart. You must agree to be a disciple of God's word, do not only listen to his word, transform his words into your lifestyle, read God's word daily, so you will not be deceived by the world's ways. **(James 1:22) "But be ye doers of the word, and not hearers only, deceiving your own selves."** All scripture are given to inform you of God's character, his words will give you the knowledge to get wealth, to be in good health, and to live a respectful life. Understand the divisions between the old and new covenant testaments in the Bible. You have to read the whole Bible to know who is speaking and learn God's standards. **(2nd Timothy 3:16) "All scripture is given by inspiration of God, and is profitable for doctrine, for reproof, for correction, for instruction in righteousness."** He wanted his people to live holy, set apart from the world's ways and rely only on him. God sent his only son into this world not to condemn this world; but to save you from condemnation. Jesus is the son of God, his message was to give grace and mercy to sinners, because we are all born sinners and needed to be protected from our sins. Jesus's death caused for a new covenant, he is the intercessor, his death for the redemption for sins, that we were under the written law, whoever believes in

Jesus, could receive the inheritance of eternal life. The testament was forced after the death of Jesus; the world received his inheritance, a new covenant how God loves you unconditionally.

(Hebrew 9:15, 17) "And for this cause he is the mediator of the new testament, that by means of death, for the redemption of the transgressions that were under the first testament, they which are called might receive the promise of eternal inheritance. For a testament is of force after men are dead: otherwise it is of no strength at all while the testator live." The Mosaic laws were given to the Jews only, it should not have been exploited to other nationalities. All other ethnic minorities were put under God's gospel of grace, and to have faith in Jesus Christ's salvation not the Mosaic laws. This is why Jesus's death; his gospel of grace took the place of God's laws to cover sins in this world. **(Acts 15:7-9) "And when there had been much disputing, Peter rose up, and said unto them, Men *and* brethren, ye know how that a good while ago God made choice among us, that the Gentiles by my mouth should hear the word of the gospel, and believe. And God, which knoweth the hearts, bare them witness, giving them the Holy Ghost, even as *he did* unto us; And put no difference between us and them, purifying their hearts by faith."** Thank you, God, for sending Jesus into the world to save the entire human race with the gospel of grace, faith and the Holy Ghost Spirit. **(Romans**

5:19) "For as by one man's disobedience many were made sinners, so by the obedience of one shall many be made righteous." You were born a sinner because of Adam and Eve's disobedience, but Jesus Christ paid the price for your righteousness. If you don't understand God's blueprint (the bible) and his purpose for your life, you will have hardship on this earth. I'm not saying if you find his purpose in your life and keep his words you will not have tribulations. When trials, tribulations, and temptations come, be joyful, Jesus overcame this world for you. If you apply God's words to your life it will comfort and cover you like a blanket. **(John 16:33) "These things I have spoken unto you, that in me ye might have peace. In the world ye shall have tribulation: but be of good cheer; I have overcome the world."** Standing on God's word, this will allow you to pay contribution to him.

When you live anyway you want to live without consulting with God, that's robbing and stealing from God. Your life does not belong to you when you became a child of God. You were created to worship God, he is a jealous God, and he will not share you with any other gods in the world. It is vital that you find the gifts God put inside you.

Ask God to reveal his path, and purpose in your life. Go back to the true meaning of God's words before you will see the full victories God has stored for your life. **(1st Corinthians 2:9) "But as it is written, Eye hath not seen, nor ear heard, neither have entered into the heart of man, the things which God hath prepared for them that love him."** Finding God's assignment for your life in this world, is the most important thing to do in your lifetime on earth.

STUDYING GOD'S WORDS

When you study the Bible, separating the words of God, Jesus, and rightfully dividing the Old and New Testaments. Both spoke different on how to live and love your neighbors. **(Hebrew 4:12) "For the word of God is quick, and powerful, and sharper than any two-edged sword, piercing even to the dividing asunder of soul and spirit, and of the joints and marrow, and is a discerner of the thoughts and intents of the heart."** God had the level of love above natural human capability, he knew that after Adam and Eve's disobedience, the world couldn't love him or others the way he wanted them to love. God created the Mosaic laws based on the world's sinful actions after sin came into the world. **(Leviticus 24:20-21) "Breach for breach, eye for eye, and tooth for tooth: as he hath caused a blemish in a man, so shall it be done to him again. And he that killeth a beast, he shall restore it: and he that killeth a man, he shall be put to death."**

Thank God, he sent Jesus into the world to introduce the gospel of grace, and the Holy Ghost Spirit. Jesus said love everyone, resist evil, turn away from wrath, help your haters, and pray for them that abuse you, and pray for people who illegally bring a lawsuit or sue you in court. Jesus had the level of love higher than your own happiness. **(Matthew 5:44) "But I say unto you, Love your enemies, bless them that curse you, do good to them that hate you, and pray for them which despitefully use you, and persecute you."** The actions of love will always be a winner whenever you are being mistreated. It is unholy to be under God's grace and still sin willfully. Only God can judge you, allow God to handle all transgressions in your life. It will be terrifying to stand at the foot of God and not be covered under Jesus's gospel of grace and mercy. **(Hebrew 10: 29- 31) "Of how much sorer punishment, suppose ye, shall he be thought worthy, who hath trodden under the Son of God, and hath counted the blood of the covenant, wherewith he was sanctified, an unholy thing, and hath done despite unto the Spirit of grace? For we know him that hath said, Vengeance belongeth unto me, I will recompense, saith the Lord. And again, The Lord shall judge his people: It is a fearful thing to fall into the hands of the living God."** Jesus's words were love your neighbors, his message was true on how God loves you. You must have faith in him to retrieve his mercy, and the gospel of grace. **(Romans 5:20-21) "Moreover the law entered, that the offence might abound. But where sin abounded, grace did much more abound: That as sin hath reigned unto death, even so might grace reign through righteousness unto eternal life by Jesus**

Christ our Lord." Grace is allowing a negative situation to enter into your life, and you are responding with full understanding that Jesus died in your place. Without the Holy Ghost Spirit of God, you will never love anyone more than yourself. **(Titus 2:11-12) " For the grace of God that bringeth salvation hath appeared to all men, Teaching us that, denying ungodliness and worldly lusts, we should live soberly, righteously, and godly, in this present world."** Grace is not a license to sin, I repeat again, grace is not a license to sin, it was given to you; because God loves you and the world could not live up to God's standards.

It's important to correctly acknowledge who is speaking when you are studying the Bible. The Bible has a beginning, middle, and ending. Words from God, Jesus, prophets, and disciples. God spoke directly to people in the beginning; he spoke to Adam and Eve, they were given all authority over the entire world. Their instructions were not to have knowledge of evil and they failed, they allowed Satan to trick them and brought sin into the world. God made plans to put an end to corruption and violence on the earth. God told Noah to build an ark to save his family from the flood. God regretted he had made human life, he destroyed the earth by flood because of sins in the world. **(Genesis 6:6) "And it repented the LORD that he had made man on the earth, and it grieved him at his heart."** After the flood, God made a new covenant with the people on earth, God stated he will not destroy the earth again by flood. God's new covenant was that he would send a rainbow from heaven inside the clouds, this was God's only covenant between him and the people, a rainbow in the sky. **(Genesis 9:8-9, 13) "And God spoke unto Noah, and to his sons with him, saying. And I, behold, I establish my covenant with you, and with your seed after you; I do set my bow in the cloud, and it shall be for a token of a covenant between me and the earth."** God told Abraham to trust and have faith in him. God introduced to Abraham how he wanted the world to love by having faith in him. God commanded Abraham to circumcise every male that was born, this was a covenant between God and the people. God counted Abraham as his friend, because he had faith and loved God.

God spoke to Moses to lead his people out of bondage into the promise land with God's laws. The prophets had an assignment to teach God's standards. The disciple's assignment was to live their life modeling God's character. I can only imagine God is hurting, to see his children have lost their way again. I thank him; because he has given all power to Jesus who had pardoned everyone for the sins in this world.

You have to focus on the ending of the Bible scriptures, the New Testament were God gave his son Jesus all authority through his death. You have the same authority Adam and Eve had in the

Garden of Eden before they lost it to Satan. God's new covenant he made with you, he stated no evil or sinful nature in this world will stop God from loving and blessing you; if you believe in Jesus Christ and stay in love. This is why the devil has no power, he was openly defeated losing the authority over you being punished for your sins and sickness and death in the spirit when Jesus died. **(Roman 8:38-39) "For I am persuaded, that neither death, nor life, nor angels, nor principalities, nor powers, nor things present, nor things to come, No height, nor depth, nor any other creature, shall be able to separate us from the love of God, which is in Christ Jesus our Lord."** God's love for you will never decrease; nothing you can do will make him stop loving you, if you honor his son Jesus.

The love God has shown you, I will question who would want to follow the devil, and his demonic demons in this world, when God has given you the gospel of grace. Jesus's death canceled out your works regarding what you must do for God to love or provide for you. Love is the only commandment God told you to do, and love is a feeling that required your emotions to care for others. God will make sure everyone knows him, it will be up to you to acknowledge him, and his son Jesus in this world.

(Hebrew 8:11-13) "And they shall not teach every man his neighbour, and every man his brother, saying, Know the

20

Lord: for all shall know me, from the least to the greatest. For I will be merciful to their unrighteousness, and their sins and their iniquities will I remember no more. In that he saith, a new covenant, he hath made the first old. Now that which decayed and waxed old is ready to vanish away." God created a new covenant between his people, the law of love, the Ten Commandments he terminated. The only commandments God told you to do is to love him first, and love others second; love is the fulfillment of God's laws.

(Matthew 22: 37-40) "Jesus said unto him, Thou shalt love the Lord thy God with all thy heart, and with all thy soul, and with all thy mind. This is the first and great commandment. And the second is like unto it, Thou shalt love thy neighbor as thyself. On these two commandments hang all law and the prophets." Clearly it's all about God's love that canceled out the Ten Commandments, and sins in this world. God loved you so much he sacrificed Jesus; his death costs you to lose your life. Your life on this earth does not belong to you, when you accept Jesus as your savior, you belong to God. I can boldly say God's words, if you decide to deny Jesus as the son of God, then you are allowing your spirit to belong to the devil in hell.

FIGHT IN THE SPIRIT

We wrestle not against flesh and blood but against demonic spirits that rule this world, wicked spirits in high places, the devil and his demons. The devil was removed from heaven, he lives in the spiritual world. Jesus is at the right hand of God in heaven, he is directing his angels to block the devil; the fight is still in the spiritual world transforming into earth. There are three worlds, Heaven, a spiritual world not seen, and the natural world you see. The fight is in the spiritual world, we live in the natural world. Your body is carnal, made of flesh and blood, you have a spirit that's made from God. **(Galatians 5:16) "This I say then, Walk in the Spirit, and ye shall not fulfil the lust of the flesh."** Sickness, death, and poverty are in the spiritual world; this is where the devil transforms his evil into earth.

You have to trust in God, lean not to your own understanding and he will redirect satanic actions in your path. God defeated the devil, he sent Jesus into the world with his spirit to give your spirit immortality on earth. God gave you the Holy Ghost Spirit, power of love, gospel of grace, and the resurrection of Jesus, these are the greatest weapons to fight the devil. The devil cannot love, his actions will always be to hate everyone that loves God. The spirit of God left him when he thought he was a god. The devil forgot he cannot be a true god and hate what God created, that is you. The weapon of your warfare is not carnal, but mighty through God pulling down strong holds, you have to cast down all thoughts and actions against the words of God.

Walk in love, faith, integrity and righteousness, because there is a demonic spirit (the devil) strolling the earth, looking to see who his demons can possess; taking over your body, soul, and spirit. **(1st Peter 5:8) "Be sober, be vigilant; because your adversary the devil, as a roaring lion, walking about, seeking whom he may devour."**

Use God's words has a shield so you can block the devil spirit that will come against you. God gave you the Holy Ghost Spirit, the power of Jesus, there is power in his name, every demon, and the devil has assigned to you has to flee from you when you call Jesus's name. **(Ephesians 6:11) "Put on the whole armor of God, that ye may be able to stand against the wiles of the devil."** The devil has no power only the power you give him.

Your life was saved when Jesus died, and he paid the price for sins, sickness, and death on the cross at Calvary. God gave you immortality; he canceled out spiritual death with a guaranteed placement in heaven. Have faith in what God gave up to free you from your sins. Jesus was given the keys to heaven and hell from God. God will send Jesus back into the world to claim his kingdom on earth. He will overthrow the devil and his demonic spirits that have been harassing you. The devil will be put into his rightful place; the lake of fire (hell). Lucifer (the devil) was a fallen angel and he wants you to follow him just like some of the other fallen angels from heaven have followed him. Jesus, who God made a little lower than an angel, God has crowned him king of all kings, no other name in heaven or earth is above Jesus's name. **(Psalms 8:4-5) "What is man, that thou art mindful of him? And the son of man, that thou visitest him? For thou hast made him a little lower than the angels, and hast crowned him with glory and honor."**

Everyone on earth will have to bow down and confess Jesus Christ is the son of God and those who love him will praise, worship, and salute him. God has given Jesus the name above all names, and all things given to him on earth and under heaven. **(Philippians 2:11) "And that every tongue should confess that Jesus Christ is Lord, to the glory of God the Father."** He has given Jesus dominion over all works of your hands and put everything under his feet. The devil is the biggest fool in this world, a complete loser, he lost his position in heaven that's why he is trying to make you lose your placement in heaven. Why would you give up paradise (heaven) on earth?

THE POWER OF LOVE

The commandment from God is to love everyone. Love is power; it came from God because he is love and powerful. **(1st John 4:16) "And we have known and believed the love that God hath to us. God is love; and he that dwelled in love dwelled in God, and God in him."** You will be responsible for how you love people, not how they love you. God put the level for loving others above your needs in life. Never love anyone more than God.

Loving others will cause you to forget your own feeling, it is like you don't exist anymore. This is why love is the most important feeling in life. Don't let life's tragedy cheat you out of the blessing God had prepared for your life. When you fail to love, you are allowing God's enemy, the devil, to manage your life; the devil will steal, kill, and destroy your life. It's important to confess how God gave up Jesus, his only son who died for you. Believing in God's word and having faith in Jesus will save you from hell.

This is a very important thought that should come to your mind, when a crisis enters your life. This is why you should be submissive to loving everyone without hesitation. Loving others is the requirement to inherit everlasting life with Jesus in heaven.

All glory be to God, who has loved you unconditionally through his son Jesus. Be submissive to loving everyone, you should be frightened by God; he can send your spirit to hell for eternity. **(Ephesians 5:20-21) "Giving thanks always for all things unto God and the Father in the name of our Lord Jesus Christ; submitting yourselves one to another in the fear of God."** Love has always been the keys, and heaven is the door.

The only debt you will ever owe is loving another person, you cannot pay off the debt of loving your neighbors. Your rewards would be in heaven because true love comes from heaven not from this world.

Seek to find the love God has for you in all relationships, people who truly love God will be your best protector in this world. The love God has for you is sufficient enough to offer love to all of your relationships in life. Knowing without any shadow of doubting that God loves you unconditionally through his son Jesus. Do not let life's tragedies shape your life in this world.

God's nature is love; he created you from love and he removed sin in your spirit by the blood of Jesus Christ. If you truly love God, you will walk in the Holy Ghost Spirit loving others 24 hours every day. This world is full of sins, and pure hate, you showing up with love will set the stage for God to be invited into your life. Walking in love to advance God's kingdom shows God you are ready to inherit heaven. Heaven is the most desirable place you should want to go when you exit from the world.

LOVING YOUR NEIGHBOR

God wants you to love without putting yourself in front, middle or end of all situations in life. Love with patient, forgiving, sharing, caring and giving; allowing everyone to be first in your life as God put you first.

When love is in the air, the room is brighter, no need for you to exit from a room full of love. Make sure you are loving with all of your heart and mind, loving your neighbor the same way God loves you, unconditionally. Love does not have a price tag because it's a feeling that God puts in you. You can't sell or purchase love, it is a spirit that God put inside your emotions.

God loved the world he created, he sent his only son to save your life from hell. Jesus died because of sins in the world. His death gave your spirit immortality; if you believe in Jesus, you have eternal life. **(John 3:16) "For God so loved the world, that he gave his only begotten Son, that whosoever believeth in him should not perish, but have everlasting life."** There is no greater love than you to lay down your life or feelings for another person. If you say you love this world and things that are in the world or have hate in your heart, the love of God is not in you.

Material things in this world are the lust of the flesh, and the pleasure of your own life, everything in this world is not of God. **(1st John 2:15-16) "Love not the world, neither the things that are in the world. If any man love the world, the love of the Father is not in him. For all that is in the world, the lust of the flesh, and the lust of the eyes, and the pride of life, is not of the Father, but is of the world."**

You have to love and judge life in the spirit of God, not in the human mind. The level of love you have for God will show how you love others. How much do you honestly love God? Love is always saying I'm sorry, forgiving without analyzing every situation in your life. No matter what is happening in your life, do not allow yourself to feel any feeling other than love.

God loves you unconditional no matter what you have done to yourself or what you did to others, he cannot stop loving you. You were built with the same kind of love in your spirit to love everyone. When you have fear, you are not walking in perfect love. If you have fear, you have stepped into your own pride, and love will not be shown with your pride. Love is like heaven on earth. God is love; that is his character; we are made from his character. God has the final judgement, allow God to judge people in this world, you can have an opinion only if you are using God's words.

Whoever you judge, you will be judged, and whatever you limit, you will be limited. Do not be prejudice to others, so you won't be judgmental. **(Matthew 7:1-2) "Judge not, that ye be not judged. For with what judgment ye judge, ye shall be judged: and with what measure ye mete, it shall be measured to you again."** Keeping your thoughts pure, leading your life with the full understanding of loving everyone at all times. Loving your neighbors more than yourself would require the spirit of God dwelling in you. The Holy Spirit is from God, he put his spirit into everyone. If you seek love, it will benefit your life greatly; love is more than having millions of dollars in the bank. Love is a free feeling that came directly from God.

EMOTIONS

When love is shown, all good emotions will be involved, the feeling is like you physically seeing God. Hate is the opposite of love; hating is like you physically seeing the devil. Love will always be the winner in every negative situation, its positive thoughts and actions. Do not allow the devil to steal your place in heaven by allowing yourself to hate. Choose to love everyone not just people who only love you. Be careful on how you treat a stranger, you could be entertaining an angel.

Purify your soul to love everyone other than yourself, don't put your needs in front of others, this is a sure way to see if you are walking in love. Loving your neighbors the same way you love your mother, father, children, and family members. This will require you to put away your own thoughts about loving others not in your family. **(Matthew 5:46) "For if ye love them which love you, what reward have ye? do not even the publicans the same?"** This is why God commanded you to love him first and others second. God's commandments will reassure you to put your feelings last in every situation around you.

LOVE

Walking in love not knowing an individual, sharing the love God has shown you is great. God knew that if you think of yourself more than others, you will make a decision on your own needs not the needs of others, and this is an action of being selfish. When you fall out of love at any point of your life, this is where you are capable of killing, stealing, cheating, and being dishonest poisoning your soul (the heart).

Love protects your soul, it's like a bulletproof vest that guards your heart. Love is an emotion that makes you feel good, it's like having a happy birthday every day. Do you want to feel like it is your birthday every day?

When there is pain, your emotions have a lot to do with your own thoughts first, you will have to train your thoughts to consult with God's word first. You have to be careful not to let life's disappointments and this world control how you are feeling. God is still in control, trust in him when trials and tribulations come into your life. Think for a moment if you allowed hate into your heart after a crisis—the spirit of the devil is controlling you. Love people, not this world or the things that are in the world, for everything in this world is temporary, will get old, and deteriorate. Hold on to loving a person, not things in the world.

LABOR IN LOVE

Laboring in love is the best workout plan in life. The Holy Spirit put love in your natural mind, allowing you to love the way God loves you. Call on the name of Jesus and be perfect in him and deny your own emotions. Become as a child, be submissive to God, be meek, and humble yourself to the words of God for love. What you do for God is only going to count in your life, not how you please yourself in this world. God is not unrighteous, he will not forget your labor of love or act of kindness to your neighbors.

Having a reputation of love will get you access to God's promises quickly, and a seat in paradise (heaven) on earth. Now is a good time to ask yourself if you want to go to heaven or hell? Heaven is for people that love others, hell is for haters. Love is the spiritual fulfilment for the kingdom! Love is the Holy Spirit inspired by God who loved you. Become a living self-sacrifice, you must be willing to agree that your life does not belong to you if you accepted Jesus as your savior. Believe that God will direct your way in life, if you ask him, and in all crisis in life have faith that he will protect you. **(Proverb 3:5) "Trust in the LORD with all thine heart; and lean not unto thine own understanding."** Every decision you make in life, God will make sure it is going to work out, if you love God, and you are working in his assignment. **(Romans 8:28) "And we know that all things work together for good to them that love God, to them who are the called according to his purpose."** God will make everything you have experienced, bad or good, work for his good.

Physical death can be hard to overcome, without the knowledge of eternal life that God gave you when Jesus died for you. Emotions can get sad or run crazy when someone you love is murdered or dies of an illness. Challenge all negative emotions into love and forgive all transgressions against you in life. Don't allow yourself to feel hate, quickly forgive, take control over your negative thoughts. Jesus's death paid for everyone's transgressions against you in this world. Do not allow sadness to overtake your thoughts when you lose a loved one.

All children who had lost their life and die premature and taken from this world will automatically go to heaven. If a person accepted Jesus as their savior, then their spirit has eternal life, whosoever believeth in Jesus will never experience spiritual death. Love should be the only integrity you have in this life, love is the foundation of God's character. Therefore, I urge you to be merciful to your neighbors, present yourself as a living sacrifice for God and love your neighbor.

Be fruitful in the spirit with kindness, patience, peacefulness, compassion, forgiving, and be understanding; these are the actions of God. Hold on to integrity, it is the only way for you to stay in love. The right way only has one way, the wrong way has multiple ways which show no love and failure.

Love is patient, love is merciful, it does not boast, love does not hate, protect honesty, love does not anger or is selfish. The only time you should ever boast in life is how much you love God and Jesus and how much you have shown love to others. God loves you so much, he offered you a covenant through his son Jesus who died for you. He wants you to reunite with him when heaven comes to earth.

Chapter Two

JESUS GRACE

God delivered on his promise to save you from self-destruction when he told the devil that he will send his spirit to bruise his head and that the devil will bruise the heel of God's spirit (Jesus). **(Genesis 3:15) "And I will put enmity between thee and the woman, and between thy seed and her seed; it shall bruise thy head, and thou shalt bruise his heel."** God sent his son to die for you. Jesus did not consider his own feelings, he only obeyed the spirit of God to lay down his life for you. He had never met you in person, he only loved you so much he died for your sins. **(Galatians 1:4) "Who gave himself for our sins, that he might deliver us from this present evil world, according to the will of God and our Father."**

Jesus came into this world born as your savior, prince of peace, a messiah, the king of all kings, your redeemer. He was God in the flesh with the supernatural power of the Holy Spirit controlling his body, soul, and spirit. You are blessed, because Jesus laid down his life for this world. Jesus loves you and he knows who all loves him. He knew God loved him when God had asked him to die for you. If you have confessed that Jesus is your savior, you can hear his voice clearly. God loved Jesus, he told Jesus to lay down his life for you, and God had given him the capability to live for eternity. No one took Jesus's life, he laid his life down, and God gave him the power of enteral life, this is what God gave him, and commanded him to give you immortality. **(John 10:15, 18) "As the Father know me, even so know I the Father: and I lay down my life for the sheep. No man taketh it from me, but I lay it down of myself. I have power to lay it down, and I have power to take it again. This commandment have I received of my Father."** The enemy is the devil, and he is a loser, he thought by assassinating Jesus he would have complete control over you and this world. He underestimated the power of God's Son, and the love God has for you.

The devil stole your inheritance, this world, he brought physical death and sickness on earth. Jesus came into the world to give you light inside eternal life, and he restored your relationship with God and your inheritance. **(John 10:10) "The thief cometh not, but for to steal, and to kill, and to destroy: I am come that they might have life, and that they might have it more abundantly."** He is your intercessor speaking to God on your behalf in heaven. Jesus canceled out the curse of sickness and death in the spirit, he made your spirit live for eternity. His blood redeemed you from Satan (the devil). Jesus laid his life down to save your life, he died in your place. He went to hell for three days for you, he rose up with all power over this world and hell.

Jesus lived his life on earth canceling out the destruction the devil was causing in this world. He triumphed over every demonic spirit. He left full instructions for you to preach the kingdom of heaven, with repentance, heal the sick, and to cast out the devil in his name. Jesus gave you the power of authority to use his name on earth. He wanted you to know that God loves you unconditionally, and whoever believes in him will have light in their life. Jesus's death—his blood cancelled out the written ordinance, he nailed it to the cross. **(Hebrew 9:22) "And almost all things are by the law purged with blood; and without shedding of blood is no remission."** He sacrificed his life to introduce God's mercy, the gospel of grace, and his salvation through his death. Jesus told you how God saved you by having faith in him to receive an enteral life. **(John 6:43-44) "Jesus therefore answered and said unto them, Murmur not among yourselves. No man can come to me, except the Father which hath sent me draw him: and I will raise him up at the last day"**

Jesus came into this world with the gospel of grace, unconditional love, and the Holy Ghost Spirit to give your spirit immortality. The gospel of grace is from God, his words are a living water well you can drink from at any time, by reading the Bible. **(John 4:14) "But whosoever drink of the water that I shall give him shall never thirst; but the water that I shall give**

38

him shall be in him a well of water springing up into everlasting life." You will not lack wisdom or knowledge with the words of God. Heaven and earth will pass away, but his words will never end. The law was given to teach you to have faith in Jesus, after faith came into this world, you are not under the law anymore. If you are baptized and have a repentant heart for your sins; therefore, you are one with Jesus Christ taking over your thoughts allowing him to be the head of all your actions. If you have faith in Christ, you will inherit eternal life this is what God promises to you. **(Galatians 3:24-27, 29) "Wherefore the law was our schoolmaster to bring us unto Christ, that we might be justified by faith. But after that faith is come, we are no longer under a schoolmaster. For ye are all the children of God by faith in Christ Jesus. For as many of you as have been baptized into Christ have put on Christ. And if ye be Christ's, then are ye Abraham's seed, and heirs according to the promise."** The law was perfect but we could not be perfect in the law. We all needed a savior; Jesus's ministry was excellent for a better covenant with endless promises for enteral life in heaven on earth. **(Roman 6:14) "For sin shall not have dominion over you: for ye are not under the law, but under grace."**

JESUS BLOOD

You have to reject your thoughts and pick up your cross for your crown. Jesus carried your cross for you when he died for you. **(Matthew 16:24) " Then said Jesus unto his disciples, if any man will come after me, let him deny himself, and take up his cross, and follow me."** Jesus's death paid the price for your freedom to serve God. He has prepared a place for you in heaven on earth, all of the angels are praising and worshipping God giving honor to God and Jesus daily. His death gave you salvation and access to God, through his blood. God has forgiven you for all of your present, past, and future sins. Jesus's death canceled out all generational curses, you have to cast down every satanic attack against you and your family by the blood of Jesus Christ.

Set your mind on miracles coming through the Holy Spirit from heaven. Jesus did his first miracle, he changed water into wine at a wedding. **(John 2:7, 9) "Jesus said unto them, fill the water pots with water. And they filled them up to the brim. When the ruler of the feast had tasted the water that was made wine, and knew not whence it was: (but the servants which drew the water knew) the governor of the feast called the bridegroom."** You can perform miracles with the Holy Ghost Spirit dwelling inside you. Jesus transformed a miracle with five loaves, and two fishes to feed the multitude of people.

Everyone was filled to their capacity, and there were remaining baskets full of fishes and bread leftover. **Matthew (14:19-21) "And he commanded the multitude to sit down on the grass, and took the five loaves, and the two fishes, and looking up to heaven, he blessed, and brake, and gave the loaves to his disciples, and the disciples to the multitude. And they did all eat, and were filled: and they took up of the fragments that remained twelve baskets full. And they that had eaten were about five thousand men, beside women and children."** He supplied food for a large crowd, by a miracle, he prayed to God to feed everyone.

Jesus's disciple cut off the ear of a soldier, Jesus laid hand on his ear, and reconstructed the soldier's ear with his touch. **(Luke 22:50-51) "And one of them smote the servant of the high priest, and cut off his right ear. And Jesus answered and said, Suffer ye thus far. And he touched his ear, and healed him."** He had performed surgery without surgical instruments. Everywhere Jesus went, he performed miracles, he had the spirit of God in his spirit; the Holy Ghost Spirit.

Jesus was talking to a demonic spirit that was inside a man. The demon was scared, he knew Jesus had the Holy Ghost Spirit, the authority and ability to terminate his evil spirit inside the man. **(Mark 1:23-26) "And there was in their synagogue a man**

with an unclean spirit; and he cried out. Saying, Let *us* alone; what have we to do with thee, thou Jesus of Nazareth? art thou come to destroy us? I know thee who thou art, the Holy One of God. And Jesus rebuked him, saying, Hold thy peace, and come out of him. And when the unclean spirit had torn him, and cried with a loud voice, he came out of him." Jesus removed the devil's demonic spirits that were handicapping people. He went throughout the world healing deformed people who had a mental and physical disability. **(Mark 8: 22, 25) "And he cometh to Bethsaida; and they bring a blind man unto him, and besought him to touch him. After that he put *his* hands again upon his eyes, and made him look up: and he was restored, and saw every man clearly."** Jesus restored eye sight to a blind man. He gave up the Spirit of the Holy Ghost when he died on the cross at Calvary. **(Luke 23:46) "And when Jesus had cried with a loud voice, he said, Father, into thy hands I commend my spirit: and having said thus, he gave up the ghost."** Ask God, in the name of Jesus for the Holy Ghost Spirit to come upon you so you will receive the same power he had to guide your life on this earth. Jesus left the spirit of the Holy Ghost Spirit to his disciples to perform the same miracles he did on earth. You have the supernatural power in your spirit to cast out the devil and his demonic spirits in your life in this world.

JESUS WORD

The world's religions have made God's words custom in a ritual tradition ceremony of preaching, practicing and performing the Mosaic laws instead of teaching Jesus's gospel of grace. **(Mark 7:13) "Making the word of God of none effect through your tradition, which ye have delivered: and many such like things do ye."** This world should only be listening to the gospel of grace message. Jesus's gospel of grace was from God. His preaching went throughout the whole world teaching how to live for the kingdom in heaven on earth. He demonstrated kingdom living, his message was to have faith in his birth, death, resurrection; love is the fulfillment of God's written law.

Some Jews, Pharisees, and Sadducees in the early church were living under the Mosaic law, they refused to believe that Jesus was God's son, and rejected the gospel of grace messages he spoke into this world. The chief priests, Sadducees, and the Pharisees dismissed Jesus's preaching, their hearts were controlled by the devil and greed they both wanted the position God gave Jesus. The devil crucified Jesus; he did not want the message of how God loves you unconditionally to spread and manifest into this world. The devil and chief priests want you to earn your inheritance and your salvation, by your works.

The devil didn't want you to have knowledge of your inheritance being transferred back to you that he stole from Adam and Eve. **(John 11:47-48, 50) "Then gathered the chief priests and the Pharisees a council, and said, what do we? for this man doeth many miracles. If we let him thus alone, all men will believe on him: and the Romans shall come and take away both our place and nation. Nor consider that it is expedient for us, that one man should die for the people, and that the whole nation perish not."** The chief priests and the Pharisees in council, did not want to lose the power they had over the people. God had given Jesus all power over this world, and Jesus gave you the power of authority to use his name in this world. Have faith in Jesus and his resurrection to receive the supernatural Holy Ghost Spirit from God. If you confessed that Jesus is your savior, your life doesn't belong to you anymore: but if you lose your life for Jesus, you will be saved by God. **(Luke 9:24) "For whosoever will save his life shall lose it: but whosoever will lose his life for my sake, the same shall save it."** Trust in God who sent Jesus into this world to save you from hell.

The works Jesus did on earth, he said greater work that you will do; by the Holy Ghost Spirit; because he is going into heaven, and whatever you ask in his name, God will do it to glorify him on earth. **(John 14:12) "Verily, verily, I say unto you, He that**

44

believeth on me, the works that I do shall he do also; and greater works than these shall he do; because I go unto my Father." Jesus left his keys to the kingdom. You have the ability to live a supernatural life with the Holy Ghost Spirit living inside you.

Quickly agree with everyone, so God will grant whatever you asked him, if two or more gather in agreement, you will see God's heart in your arrangement. You must have faith in God to remove all obstacles in your life. **(Matthew 18:19-20) "Again I say unto you, that if two of you shall agree on earth as touching any thing that they shall ask, it shall be done for them of my Father which is in heaven. For where two or three are gathered together in my name, there am I in the midst of them."** You must be borne again of the water baptism (repentance) and spirit of the Holy Ghost Spirit to inherit the kingdom of God. Whatever is born of the flesh is flesh; and whoever is born in the spirit is of the spirit, you are saved by grace, a gift from God. **(2nd Corinthians 5:17) "Therefore if any man *be* in Christ, *he is* a new creature: old things are passed away; behold, all things are become new."** If you are in Christ, you are a different person; the old you passed away.

Make sure you clean out all of the commotion in your own life before giving out your opinion. Don't be a hypocrite. First cast out the disorder of your own life, so you can see clearly to cast out the turmoil in your neighbor's life. **(Matthew 7:3-4) "And why beholdest thou the mote that is in thy brother's eye, but considerest not the beam that is in thine own eye? Or how wilt thou say to thy brother, Let me pull out the mote out of thine eye; and, behold, a beam is in thine own eye?"** Clear out the disturbance in your life before you give out any advice.

Jesus established his church on God's gospel of grace and unconditional love. You were given Jesus's kingdom keys, and his authority to rebuke the devil and his demons. The devil and hell will not win against the church. **(Matthew 16:18-19) "And I say also unto thee, that thou art Peter, and upon this rock I will build my church; and the gates of hell shall not prevail against it. And I will give unto thee the keys of the kingdom of heaven: and whatsoever thou shalt bind on earth shall be bound in heaven: and whatsoever thou shalt loose on earth shall be loosed in heaven.**" The church was built on the five-fold ministries for the work of the ministry, to teach the people how to live for the kingdom of God. **(Ephesians 4:11-12) "And he gave some, apostles; and some, prophets; and some, evangelists; and some, pastors and teachers; For the perfecting of the saints, for the work of the ministry, for the edifying of the body of Christ."** Jesus is coming back for his church, not the building, but a spirit that is in a body with his spirit in their heart. **(Matthew 24:14) "And this gospel of the kingdom shall be preached in all the world for a witness unto all nations; and then shall the end come."**

If anyone preaches any other gospel than the gospel of grace, let them be doomed. God sent Jesus into the world to die for all sins in this world, it is not by your works but through faith, and through the blood of Jesus you have received the gospel of grace from God who now loves you unconditionally. **(Galatians 1: 6, 9) "I marvel that ye are so soon removed from him that called you into the grace of Christ unto another gospel: As we said before, so say I now again, if any man preach any other gospel unto you than that ye have received, let him be accursed."** When you are preaching, who are you trying to persuade, people or God? If you pleased people then you are not Jesus's servant.

The religion of the early church, the nonbeliever, Gentiles, some Jews, Pharisees, Scribes, and Sadducees—they excluded Jesus. The religion leaders only wanted the people to follow the Ten Commandments. They prohibited to have faith in God's gospel of grace; because their minds were influenced by the devil. The devil did not want the world to know the power of the Holy Ghost Spirit, and the gospel of grace.

Jesus's disciples were given the Holy Ghost spirit to remove the devil and his demons, they healed the sick and raised people from the dead. **(Matthew 10:7-8) "And as ye go, preach, saying, The kingdom of heaven is at hand. Heal the sick, cleanse the lepers, raise the dead, cast out devils: freely ye have received, freely give."** The reason you are not witnessing that supernatural Holy Spirit power today with some of Jesus's disciples, and some churches persistently and constantly is because the true gospel of grace is being mixed with the world's ways, and the world unbelief to performing the power of the supernatural Holy Spirit. Jesus left this world with a comforter, the Holy Ghost Spirit that will teach you all things in the spirit of his words, and the spirit of truth for you to be a witness. **(Mark 16:15, 17-19) "And he said unto them, Go ye into all the world, and preach the gospel to every creature. And these signs shall follow them that believe; In my name shall they cast out devils; they shall speak with new tongues; They shall take up serpents; and if they drink any deadly thing, it shall not hurt them; they shall lay hands on the sick, and they shall recover. So then after the Lord had spoken unto them, he was received up into heaven, and sat on the right hand of God."**

You shall receive the Holy Ghost Spirit to be a witness of Jesus Christ when you are speaking the true gospel of grace over the earth, and in your life. You have the same spirit to raise the dead, heal the sick, and remove the devil and his demonic spirits inside your spirit.

When you teach or preach the gospel of grace, you must believe in Jesus Christ to receive the Holy Ghost Spirit. The spirit of God is dwelling in you when you believe in your heart and confess with your mouth that Jesus is the son of God, with the repentance of your sins. **(Roman 10: 9) "That if thou shalt confess with thy mouth the Lord Jesus, and shalt believe in thine heart that God hath raised him from the dead, thou shalt be saved."** You must have faith in what Jesus did when he went to the cross and died for you. Jesus's death gave you dominion over the devil and death. You were given immortality in your spirit, thank you, Jesus, you don't have to worry about spiritual death with the confession Jesus is your Lord and Savior.

Do not allow physical death to overcome your emotions, death is not permanent for a child of God. You have a spirit made to live for eternity in heaven or hell. Jesus left you his spirit, the Holy Ghost Spirit he gave up after he was taken from this earth. The spirit of the Holy Ghost will defeat the devil.

You are a new person with the Holy Spirit living inside you, and dead to this world, when you decided to live in the spirit, loving God, and believe in Jesus by renewing your mind daily with God's words. **(John 5:17, 47) "But Jesus answered them, My Father worketh hitherto, and I work. But if ye believe not his writings, how shall ye believe my words?"**

JESUS COVENANT

Jesus came into this world so you can have a life (Zoe) that is Christ-like on earth. He wants you to know the kingdom of heaven is in your hands. He is with God in heaven preparing to come back into this world to transform it into heaven. The devil will be destroyed, put away into hell with no return. Do not lose your confidence, for it does have great reward if you believe Jesus is coming back to claim this world. Jesus's Second coming will bring everything with him from heaven down to earth.

(John 14:1-2) "Let not your heart be troubled: ye believe in God, believe also in me. In my Father's house are many mansions: if *it were* not *so*, I would have told you. I go to prepare a place for you." If you never own a mansion be prepared to live in one in a blink of his eye you will become a zillionaire. Paradise on earth without death, sickness, and poverty. You will have the spirit of God dwelling in your body with the supernatural Holy Spirit in your mind and body permanently. Jesus was taking his last supper with his disciples, he was preparing them for his death. **(Luke 22:19-20) "And he took bread, and gave thanks, and brake *it*, and gave unto them, saying, this is my body which is given for you: this do in remembrance of me. Likewise also the cup after supper,**

saying, this cup *is* the new testament in my blood, which is shed for you." When you are eating, drinking and taking communion with Jesus, these actions will allow you to thank him for dying in your place at the cross on Calvary. Jesus's death gave this world a New Testament God's gospel of grace. Wait on heaven, do not allow your life to be stressful, it is important to have faith in Jesus's return. He promises you his kingdom will come, and it will be done on earth as in heaven.

You will have eternal life on earth, Jesus had to die for you to inherit the heaven on earth. His precious blood paid the way for you to enter into heaven. The only thing you need to do now is to keep your faith in Jesus returning to this world to make heaven on earth.

Don't give up your placement in heaven by refusing to confess or question whether Jesus was the son of God and if there is a God. Look to inherit heaven, only focus on enteral life Jesus offers through his resurrection. Inquire advancement, and you will retrieve, look, you will discover, speak God's word, and the door will unfold. **(Matthew 7:7) "Ask, and it shall be given you; seek, and ye shall find; knock, and it shall be opened unto you:"** Jesus said, if you ask for anything in his name, it shall be given to you to glorify him by God from heaven. Jesus's name is a blanket that covers your thought, do not go uncovered without seeking his mercy and the gospel of grace in your life. His covenant is guaranteed approved by God. He rightfully put you back into the grace of God. Jesus inherited this world from God, and he gave the world to you. This world is your inheritance through the bloodline of Adam, Eve, Abraham, and Jesus. God's covenant gave them this whole world. Jesus's death purchased you back from Satan, who tricked Adam and Eve to give him this world. Take back what Satan took by forcing the power of authority Jesus gave you; he left everything in this world to you before he went into heaven.

CALL INTO HEAVEN

Read the Bible scriptures carefully in this order regarding entering into heaven: **(1st Thessalonians 4:13-17), (Revelation 20:4-6, (Revelation 20:12), (Revelation 20:13-15), (Revelation 20:3, 10).** These scriptures will not line up with the world's movies or television shows, or the theories of some people.

The (unbelievers) who are called first will be judged for denying Jesus Christ, they will be removed from earth first. **(Revelation 21:2) "And I John saw the holy city, new Jerusalem, coming down from God out of heaven, prepared as a bride adorned for her husband."** A new heaven and earth is coming. If you are a believer in Jesus's birth, death and his resurrection, this scripture is saying don't be ignorant concerning those who are sleeping. People who have no hope, lost their faith in Jesus or don't believe in God, and those who worship the devil are considered sleeping; they refused the full knowledge of God and his son Jesus.

Those who believe in Jesus and waiting for his return, shall not prevent those who are considered sleeping (dead) in Christ coming into heaven, they will have a chance to enter into heaven after judgement. This is the first resurrection judgement call into heaven. Scriptures stated, when Jesus returns to earth, the dead in faith of Jesus Christ and those who have worshipped the devil shall rise first leaving earth to meet Jesus in heaven. This is the first calling for judgment. The unbeliever's will be judged to live in heaven; all that was alive: Jesus's disciples will not be judged to enter into heaven. Everyone will be called to meet Jesus in heaven at the same time he is removing the (unbelievers) from earth.

When he starts judging the people that are sleeping (dead) in Christ, he will also be transforming this world into a new heaven and new earth. **(1st Thessalonians 4:13-17) "But I would not have you to be ignorant, brethren, concerning them which are asleep, that ye sorrow not, even as others which have no hope. For if we believe that Jesus died and rose again, even so them also which sleep in Jesus will God bring with him. For this we say unto you by the word of the Lord, that we which are alive and remain unto the coming of the Lord shall not prevent them which are asleep. For the Lord himself shall descend from heaven with a shout, with the voice of the archangel, and with the trump of God: and the dead in Christ shall rise first: Then we which are alive and remain shall be caught up together with them in the clouds, to meet the Lord in the air: and so shall we ever be with the Lord"** The (dead) in Christ, and all who was serving the devil will be removed from earth first and judged by (the believers) Jesus's disciples. The believers who were persecuted for being a servant of Christ will be sitting on the throne they were judging the unbelievers. Believers in Jesus, the people who did not worshipped the devil, will be judging the other people who have the mark of the beast (devil), all who were worshipping the devil and refused Jesus salvation.

Jesus's disciples would have already lived and reigned with Jesus for a thousand years in heaven. The people who did not believe in Christ and who were serving the devil will be judged according to their works on earth. Only the chosen unbelievers, after being judged will they reign with Jesus and his disciples after the one thousand years has passed. This will be the first resurrection call into heaven for non-believers in Christ.

The second death will be people who didn't need to be judged by God, Jesus Christ's disciples who had no power until Jesus transforms earth into the new heaven. The believers in Christ, they will live with him a thousand years in heaven, and they will be priests of God and Jesus.

The scripture states Jesus Christ is coming back and bringing a new heaven and earth to this world. Start preparing for his return as you never know when he will arrive. Keep his name and his words in your soul and spirit. **(Revelation 20:4-6) "And I saw thrones, and they sat upon them, and judgment was given unto them: and I saw the souls of them that were beheaded** for the witness of Jesus, and for the word of God, and which had not worshipped the beast, neither his image, neither had received his mark upon their foreheads, or in their hands; and they lived and reigned with Christ a thousand years. But the rest of the dead lived not again until the thousand years were finished. This is the first resurrection. Blessed and holy is he that hath part in the first resurrection: on such the second death hath no power, but they shall be priests of God and of Christ, and shall reign with him a thousand years."

Jesus's disciples who reigned with him a thousand years will be on the throne. They will be judging the unbelievers and the people who serve the devil. Blessed are the people that will be called first into judgment who were allowed to join the believers in Jesus Christ after the thousand years ended. The disciples will never be judged to enter into heaven, they will be God and Jesus's priests.

The (dead) in Christ and all who worshipped the devil will have to stand before God to be judged for their works on earth. God will open two books, one was the book of life. The people who did not believe in Jesus and who worshipped the devil will be judged from both books of life, and things they did on earth that were written in the book of life. (Revelation 20:12) "And I saw the dead, small and great, stand before God; and the books were opened: and another book was opened, which is the book of life: and the dead were judged out of those things which were written in the books, according to their works."

All unbeliever's in Christ, the dead buried in their grave, dead in hell will be judged according to their works. Everyone who was worshipping the devil will be cast into the lake of fire (hell). The people whose names were not written in the book of life will be cast into the lake of fire. **(Revelation 20:13-15) "And the sea gave up the dead which were in it; and death and hell delivered up the dead which were in them: and they were judged every man according to their works. And death and hell were cast into the lake of fire. This is the second death. And whosoever was not found written in the book of life was cast into the lake of fire."** This will be the final death for unbelievers.

The devil will not beguile the nation for a thousand years, and God's people will have lived and reigned with Jesus in the new heaven for those thousand years. After the thousand year's ends, the devil will be loose for a little time before going into hell. **(Revelation 20:3, 10) "And cast him into the bottomless pit, and shut him up, and set a seal upon him, that he should deceive the nations no more, till the thousand years should be fulfilled: and after that he must be loosed a little season. And the devil that deceived them was cast into the lake of fire and**

brimstone, where the beast and the false prophet are, and shall be tormented day and night for ever and ever." This is the final death for the devil, his prophets and all of the antichrist people who refused salvation from Jesus Christ will be put into hell permanently.

Movies on television falsely lead people with the presumption that the same people being taken up first from earth are going to live in heaven first. This is the world's biggest lie. When Jesus returns to earth to setup the new heaven and earth, everyone will go at the same time into their rightful position in heaven or hell.

Read the scriptures carefully; some people, the unbelievers (dead) sleeping in Jesus Christ, and the people who were worshipping the devil will be taken from earth, this is the first judgement call into heaven. These people have to be judged for their works on earth. The people whose name was in the book of life will join Jesus and his disciples after judgement and the thousand years have ended, this is when the new heaven starts reigning in this world. Jesus's servant will never be judged, they will be doing the judgement. Jesus's disciples will be God and Jesus's priests. (This is my opinion after carefully reading these scriptures) these are the most comprehensive scriptures about going into heaven. If you are practicing to keep the laws of Moses rather than Jesus's gospel of grace message; you will be judged according to Mosaic Laws. **(Matthew 7:21-23) "Not every one that saith unto me, Lord, Lord, shall enter into the kingdom of heaven; but he that doeth the will of my Father which is in heaven. Many will say to me in that day, Lord, Lord, have we not prophesied in thy name? and in thy name have cast out devils? and in thy name done many wonderful works? And then will I profess unto them, I never knew you: depart from me, ye that work iniquity."** Have faith in Jesus who fulfilled the laws of God with the only two commandments to love God and others.

The only way to inherit heaven on earth is to live your life loving everyone at all times. There is a thin line between love and hate. **(Matthew 7:13-14) " Enter ye in at the strait gate: for wide *is* the gate, and broad *is* the way, that leadeth to destruction, and many there be which go in thereat: Because strait *is* the gate, and narrow *is* the way, which leadeth unto life, and few there be that find it."** Many people will find themselves inside the line of God's judgment, because of lack of loving people at all times.

Chapter Three

ENTERAL LIFE

If you confessed Jesus is the son of God, and that God raised Jesus from the dead from the pits of hell, and with the repentance of your sins, you are saved. You will never taste spiritual death, you will experience physical death. Your body will be removed from earth. The devil can only kill the physical body, he doesn't have the power to kill a spirit made from God. Your spirit is built to live for eternity; you will live in heaven or hell. You can decide where your spirit will live for eternity. You are made of three parts as a human being. You have a body, a soul, and a spirit. You are a spirit that houses a physical body, a soul (the heart), and a spirit like God. Your body is made from human organs, your soul is your heart controlled by your mind, and your spirit is where God lives inside you. God, his son Jesus, and the Holy Ghost Spirit is one person with a spirit of a three-part trinity. God will always have full power over death and the devil.

There is testimony of resurrections of the dead preformed inside the Bible where God extended life to someone who died. God's prophet, Elijah, preformed a resurrection on a woman's son that was dead. Elijah cried out to God to bring life back into the boy's body. **(1st Kings 17:22) "And the LORD heard the voice of**

Elijah; and the soul of the child came into him again, and he revived." Elijah brought the child to his mother alive. Elisha laid hands on a dead child, and his eyes opened; the boy woke up from the dead. **(2nd Kings 4:34) "And he went up, and lay upon the child, and put his mouth upon his mouth, and his eyes upon his eyes, and his hands upon his hands: and he stretched himself upon the child; and the flesh of the child waxed warm."** Elisha restored life back into a child, he opened his eyes and sneezed. A little boy's mother was crying, Jesus told her do not weep, he touched her son, he that was dead was alive again, and started talking. **(Luke 7:14-15) "And he came and touched the bier: and they that bare *him* stood still. And he said, Young man, I say unto thee, Arise. And he that was dead sat up, and began to speak. And he delivered him to his mother."** Jesus had compassion for a mother whose son was dead.

Jesus brought life back to a maid who was dead. **(Luke 8:52-55) "And all wept, and bewailed her: but he said, Weep not; she is not dead, but sleepeth. And they laughed him to scorn, knowing that she was dead. And he put them all out, and took her by the hand, and called, saying, Maid, arise. And her spirit came again, and she arose straightway: and he commanded to give her meat."** Jesus restored life to a maid, her family was very happy to see her alive again. Jesus asked God to show the people around him that he had sent him and that he was his son, and death is temporary, for those who believe in him. **(John 11:41-44) "Then they took away the stone from the place where the dead was laid. And Jesus lifted up his eyes, and said, Father, I thank thee that thou hast heard me. And I knew that thou hear me always: but because of the people which stand by I said it, that they may believe that thou hast sent me. And when he thus had spoken, he cried with a loud voice, Lazarus, come forth. And he that was dead came forth, bound hand and foot with grave clothes: and his face was bound about with a napkin. Jesus said unto them, loose him, and let him go."** This is the most powerful act Jesus did right in front of everyone where he called Lazarus out of the grave after being dead for four days.

Jesus cried at the cross, he was dying on the cross at Calvary, taking his last earthly breath in his physical body. He released the Holy Ghost Spirit into the world, there were bodies of the disciples rising out of the grave after Jesus's death. **(Matthew 27:50, 52) "Jesus, when he had cried again with a loud voice, yielded up the ghost. And the graves were opened; and many bodies of the saints which slept arose."** Jesus spirit was going into heaven, the power of the Holy Ghost Spirit made some people rise from the dead. Jesus came out of a grave in three days, and he appeared to one of his disciples. **(Mark 16:9) "Now when Jesus was risen early the first day of the week, he appeared**

first to Mary Magdalene, out of whom he had cast seven devils." After Jesus was crucified, and buried in the grave, he had risen out of the grave, and was walking around with his disciples. **(John 20:26, 29) "And after eight days again his disciples were within, and Thomas with them:** *then* **came Jesus, the doors being shut, and stood in the midst, and said, Peace** *be* **unto you. Jesus saith unto him, Thomas, because thou hast seen me, thou hast believed: blessed** *are* **they that have not seen, and** *yet* **have believed."** Death has no power over the child of God, and a believer in Jesus Christ that knows death is temporary.

Jesus was given the authority from God to remove the power of death on earth. In your spirit, Jesus gave you the power to cast out the devil and his demonic spirits.

Heaven is coming on earth, keep your eyes on the prize. Do not let this world cheat you out of your inheritance of enteral life. The truth is you were made to live forever; your body was built to have immortality. Jesus gave you enteral life and no one can take you out of his hand nor will anyone cease that believes in Jesus. Jesus was made from the Holy Ghost Spirit, God, giving him eternal life **(John 10:28-29) "And I give unto them eternal life; and they all will never perish, neither shall any man pluck them out of my hand. My Father, which gave them me, is**

greater than all; and no man is able to pluck them out of my Father's hand." When you have confessed Jesus is the son of God with repentance of your sins, and believe in his resurrection from the dead. Eternal life is your inheritance from God. This is why Jesus died a physical death, so that you will have eternal life with him in heaven. Understanding that physical death is part of this life on earth, we have to die in our physical body to put on the spiritual body of eternal life. Remember, inside your body is a spirit that lives forever. The physical body is like a house you can fill it with many things, the soul (the heart) is where you can build up or tear down your life, your spirit is where God lives inside of you.

There are three worlds, the physical world is what you see, hear, touch and feel which affect your body. The spiritual world is where angels, devil and demons are fighting over your spirit to control your soul (the heart) this is how you are living out your life here on earth. Heaven is home for all believers in Jesus Christ, where you will live your eternal life. It's going to be paradise on earth.

Do not let the devil trick you into believing he has the power over finalizing death, because he does not have the full power, it was taken from him. When God blew breath into your nostril, he gave you eternal life. Do not worry about who can kill your body or soul (your heart), a person or the devil. Stay focused on God, he can kill the body, soul, and put your spirit in hell for eternity **(Matthew 10:28) "And fear not them which kill the body, but are not able to kill the soul: but rather fear him which is able to destroy both soul and body in hell."** You will live eternal life in hell if you do not acknowledge Jesus is the son of God. The lust of this world will pass away. Look not at things you can see, for those things that are seen are temporary, things not seen are eternal like heaven, which you cannot see now. **(John 6:63) "It is the spirit that quickeneth; the flesh profiteth nothing: the words that I speak unto you, *they* are spirit, and *they* are life."** If you sow into the flesh your body, you will reap corruption in the flesh, sow into your spirit, which is the words of God, you will reap the spirit of Jesus's everlasting life that God gave him.

The wages of sins were death but, through the blood of Jesus, you have eternal life. **(Galatians 5:18) "But if ye be led of the Spirit, ye are not under the laws."** Fight the good fight of faith look at what God gave up for you to have eternal life; he sacrificed his only son. The good news about Jesus's death is his resurrection when he rose on the third day. **(Luke 24:34, 36, 39, 46) "Saying, The Lord is risen indeed, and hath appeared to Simon. And as they thus spake, Jesus himself stood in the midst of them, and saith unto them, Peace *be* unto you. Behold my hands and my feet, that it is I myself: handle me, and see; for a spirit**

hath not flesh and bones, as ye see me have. And said unto them, Thus it is written, and thus it behoved Christ to suffer, and to rise from the dead the third day:" Jesus returned to earth from hell, he took the power of spiritual death on earth. He returned with the keys to eternal life, God gave Jesus full power over this earth, hell and heaven.

Chapter Four

DEVIL

The devil, chief priests and the scribes put a contract out on Jesus's life. They hired a hitman, one of Jesus's disciple Judas was setup to betray Jesus. **(Luke 22:2-3, 47-48) "And the chief priests and scribes sought how they might kill him; for they feared the people. Then entered Satan into Judas surnamed Iscariot, being of the number of the twelve. And while he yet spake, behold a multitude, and he that was called Judas, one of the twelve, went before them, and drew near unto Jesus to kiss him. But Jesus said unto him, Judas, betrayest thou the Son of man with a kiss?"** Judas, being possess by the devil, double-crossed Jesus for thirty pieces of silver.

The early church leaders were blind by the devil, religion laws, and their unbelief of the gospel of grace message. Because they did not believe that God sent Jesus into the world to save the world from Satan (the devil). The devil will send temptations and tribulations into your life, but God will make all trials and transgressions your testimonies. (This is my opinion on the story about Job in the Bible scriptures) It can be difficult to understanding why God allowed Satan to afflict Job, if you don't comprehend the meaning of the story. **(Job 1: 6-8) "Now there was a day when the sons of God came to present themselves** before the LORD, and Satan came also among them. And the **LORD said unto Satan, Whence comest thou? Then Satan answered the LORD, and said, From going to and fro in the earth, and from walking up and down in it. And the LORD said unto Satan, Hast thou considered my servant Job, that** *there is* **none like him in the earth, a perfect and an upright man, one that feareth God, and escheweth evil?"** God wanted you to know that he is in full control of what is happening in your life, and the devil just cannot do anything to you, without God's interference.

Job was a rich man, he loved God and feared him: he walked upright with God. In the cool of one day, God asked Satan where he was going. Satan said he was walking around earth (seeking who he can deceive). God asked, "Satan, have you considered my servant Job?" Satan told God he has blessed Job's hands and his house, if he takes his hands off of Job he will curse God to his face. **(Job 1:12) "And the LORD said unto Satan, Behold, all that he hath** *is* **in thy power; only upon himself put not forth thine hand. So Satan went forth from the presence of the LORD."** God told Satan, everything Job has is in Satan's hands now, but don't kill him. God put restrictions on Satan to interrupt Job's life. God wanted to show Satan that Job will love him unconditionally.

Job started losing his wealth, children, and friends. Job fell upon the ground, he started praising God and said, "Naked you come into this world and naked you will leave everything in the world." Job did not sin, nor did he charge God for his loss.

Job's soul (heart) was weary, he did not tell anyone his pain. In his pain he told God not to condemn him, and he questioned why God was condemning him. **(Job 13:3, 15) "Surely I would speak to the Almighty, and I desire to reason with God. Though he slay me, yet will I trust in him: but I will maintain mine own ways before him."** Job stated it was good that God oppress him and took his hands off of him, to show Satan that Job will love God no matter how bad a situation gets. Satan told God if he put sickness on Job, he will curse God to his face. Satan wanted to test Job's love for God again. He made Job sick, close to dying, and his wife said, "Why don't you curse God and die?" Job said, "You foolish woman, why would you change your love for God because of evil coming upon you?"

With all of Job's problems, he did not sin or curse God. Job's friends came to comfort him and they were mourning because he was sick. All of his friends lifted up their eyes crying, and they ripped Job's mantles and sprinkled dust on their heads and looked up toward heaven. They should have known not to speak against God. God had spoken to Job, God told Job's friends, and he was disappointed with them, because they spoke against him. God told his friends to take up a burned offering to Job, and ask Job to pray for them, so that God will forgive them for speaking against him. His friends did what God told them to do, and Job prayed for his friends, and God accept Job's prayer and forgave his friends. God gave Job double for his trouble, he had blessed him with twice as much as he had before.

The story about Job in the Bible is to let you know, do not blame God for any transgressions or get discouraged when you lose someone or somethings in this world. The devil is the responsible spirit that causes all sins, death and tribulations in this world. Through the bloodline of Jesus, everything you lost will be restored, when heaven comes on earth. Thank you, God, for sending Jesus into this world with the power of the Holy Spirit, eternal life, and the gospel of grace.

Do not lose your faith in Jesus's gospel of grace or how God loves you unconditionally. The devil wants you to earn your salvation by your works; he wants you to question the salvation Jesus gave you. The devil is the God of this world, who has blinded the mind of the true gospel of grace, in most of the world's religions today. **(2nd Corinthians 4:3-4) "But if our gospel be hid, it is hid to them that are lost: in whom the god of this world hath blinded the minds of them which believe not, lest the light of the**

glorious gospel of Christ, who is the image of God, should shine unto them." Protect your mind with God's word; it is the battleground for God or the devil to make decision in your life. God wants you to love unconditionally, the devil demands for you to hate everyone. Don't allow the devil to control your mind by walking in hate or not forgiving everyone that trespasses against you in life.

The devil is a killer, a self-destructor, a thief, and a liar; the father of lies. God did not give you the spirit of hate, it came from God's enemy, the devil. Do not underestimate the devil, he is a spirit, a fallen angel. **(Revelation 12:12) "Therefore rejoice, *ye* heavens, and ye that dwell in them. Woe to the inhabiters of the earth and of the sea! For the devil is come down unto you, having great wrath, because he knoweth that he hath but a short time."** The devil is causing situations where death came upon earth with his evil spirits and sins he has created in this world. You will never fight against a person; your fight will always be with a demonic spirit that possesses a person's soul (their heart).

The devil and his demons will try to possess leaders of all nations in this world. **(Ephesians 6:12) "For we wrestle not against flesh and blood, but against principalities, against powers, against the rulers of the darkness of this world, against**

spiritual wickedness in high places." The devil has influenced the world's laws and regulations on earth. Only God holds the power of resurrection, something the devil does not hold in his power nor does he want to behold bringing life into the world.

The devil's character is death, his disobedience to God causes sin in this world, and sin causes physical death. He lost his place in heaven, this is why he wants you to lose your place in heaven, by being disobedient and making statements that Jesus is not God's son and God didn't tell you to love him and everyone. To defeat the devil, you need to speak God's word and walk in unconditional love. Never fall out of loving others, this is protection guaranteed by God with his approval for you to be a winner in your life.

The devil hates you; his spirit is hatred, he is considered a hater. Don't fall for the oldest trick the devil is still playing and played on Adam and Eve when he told them to sin against God and that they wouldn't physically die. If you dance with the devil, he will leave you standing alone on the floor dancing; after his song stops playing, he will be gone. Do not let the devil play you like a piano, don't let him write your song.

The devil wants to cheat you out of eternal life. He wants you to join him in hell. Be very careful on how you are making decisions on earth, it will determinate where you will live out your eternal life when heaven starts reigning on earth. Knowing how much God loves you, and his words, will stop the attack of the devil.

The devil will tell you to perform the act of a sin, then leave you to die. First, listen to the voices in your mind and question your thoughts. Is it God or the devil speaking to you? Keep your thoughts on God's words. You have to open your mouth, it is okay to talk to the devil, don't let him be the only one talking to you. Jesus was tempted by the devil, and he told the devil you are not to live on food alone, but by every word God has spoken and serve God only. The devil should be behind you not inside your mind, don't give him that option. **(Matthew 4:1, 4, 10) "Then was Jesus led up of the Spirit into the wilderness to be tempted of the devil. But he answered and said, it is written, Man shall not live by bread alone, but by every word that proceedeth out of the mouth of God. Then saith Jesus unto him, Get thee hence, Satan: for it is written, Thou shalt worship the Lord thy God, and him only shalt thou serve."** You should praise, worship, and renew your mind, soul and spirit with God's words daily.

The devil has demonic spiritual power, he will send his demons to attack you when there is a doorway or window of opportunity for sins in your life. It's important to walk and talk in the light of God. When you have to hide, cheat, bare false witness, or kill, you are on the devil's payroll. Satan is self-employed and he wants you to be self-employed so you can self-destruct your own life. If you are a child of God, he hates you and would like to see you dead.

Working for the devil will put your life in chaos, he will have you thinking of yourself only. You are in for a fight for your life, whether you know it or not, the devil wants you to be ignorant on your inheritance… this world, how God loves you unconditional, and Jesus's gospel of grace. Fight the devil with God's words. The devil will trick you into sinning so he can have the right to access your life. This is why sins can cause physical death, someone or something has to die when sins take place on earth. **(James 4:7) "Submit yourselves therefore to God. Resist the devil, and he will flee from you."** Jesus gave you the Holy Ghost Spirit, this is the spirit of God. God will stop the devil in his own tracks when you are speaking God's words. The devil wants your spirit in hell with him, he can kill your physical body that is connected to your heart with your permission; he cannot kill the Spirit of God inside you.

Chapter Five

DEATH

God has given you immortality over death and sickness, don't allow your feeling to be sorrowful when death occurs on earth. The devil wants you to feel pain. Watch your character when death and sickness come into your life. These actions Satan is responsible for, and he wants you to doubt God's love for you and your family.

It's important to know that the devil is the responsible evil spirit that causes physical death and sickness in this world. Don't let the devil trick you in questioning if God loves you. **(Hebrews 2:9, 14) "But we see Jesus, who was made a little lower than the angels for the suffering of death, crowned with glory and honour; that he by the grace of God should taste death for every man. Forasmuch then as the children are partakers of flesh and blood, he also himself likewise took part of the same; that through death he might destroy him that had the power of death, that is, the devil."** God already won the war with the devil on this issue of death when he gave you eternal life.

How you defeat the devil when tragedy come into your home, start praising God for the victories he had already won, and what he is going to do. Adam was made from the earth's dirt, but Jesus was made with the Holy Ghost Spirit with an immortal body. Earth is earth, and heaven is heaven. **(1st Corinthians 15:44-45, 47) "It is sown a natural body; it is raised a spiritual body. There is a natural body, and there is a spiritual body. And so it is written, the first man Adam was made a living soul; the last Adam was made a quickening spirit. The first man is of the earth, earthy: the second man is the Lord from heaven."** Flesh and blood cannot inherit the kingdom of God; neither can corruption inherit incorruption. It is a mystery; we all shall not be sleeping (dead) in Jesus Christ, but everyone will be changed in the blink of his eye at the last trumpet: the trumpet sounded, the unbelievers in Jesus will be incorruptible and changed. **(Roman 8:7-8) "Because the carnal mind *is* enmity against God: for it is not subject to the law of God, neither indeed can be. So then they that are in the flesh cannot please God."** Everyone who believe in God and Jesus Christ will be incorruptible.

The corruption will have to put on incorruption, and this mortal body will have to put on immortality. Death will expire, you will have victory, and I question where is the power in death for those that are sleeping in the grave, who belong to Jesus? Sins were death; and sins strengthen by the law. **(1ˢᵗ Corinthians 15:20-22) "But now is Christ risen from the dead, *and* become the firstfruits of them that slept. For since by man *came* death, by man *came* also the resurrection of the dead. For as in Adam**

76

all die, even so in Christ shall all be made alive." Thank you, God, for sending Jesus Christ, who has the power of eternal life. Keep your mind on what God did, he redeemed you through the blood of Jesus who offered you full resurrection when he returns to earth.

You must stay focused on the unmovable God, always be willing to do the work for God's kingdom, know that your labor for the kingdom will not be in vain. In this world, you will have trials, temptations, and tribulations; be grateful Jesus overcame death.

(Revelation 21:4) "And God shall wipe away all tears from their eyes; and there shall be no more death, neither sorrow, nor crying, neither shall there be any more pain: for the former things are passed away." Hell is not your home, you do have a permanent home in heaven, if you accepted Jesus Christ as your savior, you are a conqueror, child of God, and greater in Jesus than in you that is in this earth. You owe God your body, soul, and spirit. **(1st John 4:4) "Ye are of God, little children, and have overcome them: because greater is he that is in you, than he that is in the world."** If you confessed Jesus is your savior, then he will become more to you than this world.

Chapter Six

MONEY

Money is a tool to purchase material things; however, love is a feeling that controls your emotions. Both have powerful statement of actions. Money shouldn't be on the same level as love. When you love everyone, you are rich in the spirit of God. **(Matthew 19:23-24) "Then said Jesus unto his disciples, Verily I say unto you, That a rich man shall hardly enter into the kingdom of heaven. And again I say unto you, It is easier for a camel to go through the eye of a needle, than for a rich man to enter into the kingdom of God."** Having money can make you feel good, the thoughts of achievement will make you possibly think you are in control over your own destiny in life.

Enjoy having fun with material things, money will pay for all things in this world. Money is a piece of paper that holds no value in loving anyone. **(Ecclesiastes 10:19) "A feast is made for laughter, and wine make merry: but money answer all things."** Everything in this world is controlled by money, you will need money to live a victorious life on earth.

You are very rich with good health. Your health and wealth come from God. Poverty and sickness come from the devil. When you make money more important than a human life or love and others happiness, you have made money sinful and the foundation of wickedness. This corruption the devil put inside your emotions of achieving material things without you sharing and caring for others. **(1st Timothy 6:10) "For the love of money is the root of all evil: which while some coveted after, they have erred from the faith, and pierced themselves through with many sorrows."** Do not let the devil put his spirit of mammon in control of your money or mind. You cannot serve God and money, you will abuse one and love the other. **(Matthew 6:24) "No man can serve two masters: for either he will hate the one, and love the other; or else he will hold to the one, and despise the other. Ye cannot serve God and mammon."** The decisions you make about handling your money will show who you're serving, God or money. Do not allow money to be more valuable than a person's life.

Your promotions do not come from north, east, not the west or south it comes from God. You were not designed to go into the world for money; the kingdom of God is self-sufficient, he will supply your needs. God will give you the knowledge to get wealth, if you are faithful over handling your money in life, God will increase your income. **(Matthew 25:20-21) "And so he that had received five talents came and brought other five talents, saying, Lord, thou deliveredst unto me five talents: behold, I have gained beside them five talents more. His lord said unto** him, well done, thou good and faithful servant: thou hast been faithful over a few things, I will make thee ruler over many things: enter thou into the joy of thy lord."

God's expectation is for you to increase the money he put into your hands. It is your responsibility to make an investment on the money God has given you, without making an investment with your money, it will result in improper handling of money.

God will bless all the works of your hands; you shall give to everyone in need, and not borrow, you should have enough money and food to share, and you shall not be overwhelmed in debt; you shall have a surplus every day and not lacking anything pertaining to your needs in life. Trust in God, he will provide for you and others. **(Deuteronomy 28:12-13) "The Lord shall open unto thee his good treasure, the heaven to give the rain unto thy land in his season, and to bless all the work of thine hand: and thou shalt lend unto many nations, and thou shalt not borrow. And the LORD shall make thee the head, and not the tail; and thou shalt be above only, and thou shalt not be beneath; if that thou hearken unto the commandments of the LORD thy God, which I command thee this day, to observe and to do them."**

It is God who will give you the power to get wealth, he will establish his covenant that he swore into you the seed of Abraham and Jesus until this day. Having God favor over your life is a blessing coming from heaven. God has put love in a person's mind to favor you. When favor is on your life, supernatural progress happens and unexplained upgrades of material things in life. The favor of God is evident from heaven showing everyone that God is blessing you on earth. **(Acts 20:35) "I have shewed you all things, how that so laboring ye ought to support the weak, and to remember the words of the Lord Jesus, how he said, It is more blessed to give than to receive."**

If God has given you an overflow of money, he is trusting you to advance the kingdom of God, spread his words throughout the world; to help take care of people living in poverty. You are blessed to be a blessing to someone in need.

Everything in heaven is elegant and free. You cannot earn your way into heaven by giving money, because heaven is not for sale. Jesus stated whoever left their family and who has given up material things for the gospel of grace shall receive a hundred percent in return now and when heaven comes. **(Mark 10:29-30) "And Jesus answered and said, Verily I say unto you, There is no man that hath left house, or brethren, or sisters, or father, or mother, or wife, or children, or lands, for my sake, and the gospel's, But he shall receive an hundredfold now in this time, houses, and brethren, and sisters, and mothers, and**

children, and lands, with persecutions; and in the world to come eternal life." You will never lose out of giving into God's kingdom. Applying God's plans, grace and mercy into your life first, and everything will be given to you by God. **(Matthew 6:33) "But seek ye first the kingdom of God, and his righteousness; and all these things shall be added unto you."** Modeling God's character in your life, you will retrieve all of Jesus's blessings. **(Luke 8:11) "Now the parable is this: The seed is the word of God."**

The parable about God's seeds, or his words, are sowed into your life. Some seeds sowed will fall on a rock, you will hear God's words with joy, but do not transform his words into your lifestyle with unbelief in temptation; you fall away from God's words.

Some seeds are sowed on thorns, you heard God's words, and you allowed life situation to block out God's words, because of the cares of being rich or your own pleasure, your life is not fruitful and you lack the patience to receive.

Some seeds sowed by the wayside, you hear God's words, you allowed the devil to take God's words away for your heart, because of lack of believing you are saved by grace.

Some seeds sowed on good ground; this is where you heard God's words and you live honestly with a good heart and keep his words to bring forth good fruit. With patience, it will bring a hundred percent in return. If you are living a Christ-like life, with a good soul (heart) and have faith in Jesus, you are sowing on good ground that can bring a hundred percent in return.

Some seeds sowed can bring sixty, other seeds sowed at thirty; the level of your faith in Jesus will determine your return.

Stop debating giving money to support God's words in his churches, he doesn't want your money, he wants you to respect his character, and to love him and others. Funding the churches should be on the highest level; therefore, it is greater than paying for a professional college degree. Learning God's words is the most important education and knowledge in this world. Heaven and earth will pass away but God's words shall not pass away. The gospel of grace is free but his words cost to translate to the entire world. This should settle all disagreement about giving money to the church to spread the kingdom of God's word into this world. God is looking at your soul (the heart) when you give out money. **(Mark 12:41-43) "And Jesus sat over against the treasury, and beheld how the people cast money into the treasury: and many that were rich cast in much. And there came a certain poor widow, and she threw in two mites, which make a farthing. And he called *unto him* his disciples, and saith unto them, Verily I say unto you, That this poor widow hath cast more in, than all they which have cast into the**

treasury." Make sure you have a charity spirit when you are contributing money to someone that is in need or to support God's kingdom.

Stay faithful, have hope and charity. Out of all three, charity would be the greatest. Keep your life from loving material things, by loving people not money, this will allow you to give freely. If you give sparing you will receive sparingly, and if you give bountifully you will receive abundantly, everyone give according to their heart, and do not give grudgingly for God loves a overgenerous giver.

If you feed your flesh, you will receive corruption; but if you feed your spirit you shall receive enteral life. **(Galatians 6:7) "Be not deceived; God is not mocked: for whatsoever a man soweth, that shall he also reap."** Do not worry, in any season in your life you will receive what you have sowed if you don't lose faith.

Some early church leaders did not want people to follow Jesus because he was preforming miracles without taking any animals sacrifices or tithes, they did not want people to stop giving money and sacrificing animals to the church. The chief priests, and religious people including the Pharisees and Sadducees had something in common with the devil, they both wanted the authority over the people and the world's money. The bottom line, Jesus was killed for money. The devil did not want you to know that Jesus came to restore your inheritance in this world. Heaven is God's home, but he gave this world to you.

Animal exchange and sacrifice was one of the ways the churches paid contribution to God. Abraham was following after his tradition and generation, paying tithes out of respect to the priesthood. He gave a 10th of his salary according to the law in the land. **(Hebrew 7:5) "And verily they that are of the sons of Levi, who receive the office of the priesthood, have a commandment to take tithes of the people according to the law, that is, of their brethren, though they come out of the loins of Abraham."**

Jesus came into the world, he changed the system of priesthood, the laws also needed to be changed. Jesus Christ's ancestors were not like the Levi ancestors who took tithing and offers from the people. For Jesus Christ was from the tribe of Judah a different generation, with no altar or priesthood to take tithes and offerings from the people. There was no need for another priesthood.

(Hebrew 7:12-14, 16, 18) "For the priesthood being changed, there is made of necessity a change also of the law. For he of whom these things are spoken pertaineth to another tribe, of which no man gave attendance at the altar. For it is evident that our Lord sprang out of Juda; of which tribe Moses spake nothing concerning priesthood. Who is made, not after the

law of a carnal commandment, but after the power of an
endless life, For there is verily a disannulling of the
commandment going before for the weakness and
unprofitableness thereof." Jesus was not a priest, he was
ministering to sinful, vulnerable, poor people, and for a non-
profitable, eternal-life message to draw people to God. The law
made nothing perfect, it brought you closer to God.

Jesus has a better covenant unchangeable and is making
intercession to God for you, Jesus is in heaven, no need to offer
sacrifice for sins anymore. He was offered up for the sins, by the
words of God, his body was consecrated forever. This explains
how Jesus's blood canceled out animal sacrifice, and how God
will love you and support you. God is blessing you, and the world
through the death of his son. **(Hebrew 7:22) "By so much was
Jesus made a surety of a better testament."**

You cannot put a price on how much God loves you. God tempted
Abraham to offer up Isaac, his son, as a human sacrifice. God was
testing Abraham on his obedience; would he be willing to
sacrifice his son who he loved for the love of God? Abraham put
his son on an altar to kill him, God's angel stopped him, and then
a lamb was provided instead of using Isaac has a human sacrifice.

Abraham passed the test, he showed God he loved him more than his son. After he passed the test, God blessed Abraham and this world because Abraham obeyed, and feared God's voice. God was showing Abraham how to love him more than a family member. God sacrificed his only son, Jesus, for the world's sins to show you how much he loves everyone. This world is blessed because of Abraham's obedience and Jesus's death. No more need to sacrifice animals or perform for God to love you; the law is love. God gave you his only son, Jesus; he died in your place.

Jesus's death paid for you to have eternal life and to have freedom from your works performing the laws, tithing, and fasting, none of these actions will get you into heaven. Only God's love and you loving others qualify you to inherit heaven, and faith in Jesus's gospel of grace canceled out your works to inherit the Kingdom of God.

The Ten Commandments are actions from the laws, God's people failed at keeping all of the laws. **(James 2:10) "For whosoever shall keep the whole law, and yet offend in one point, he is guilty of all."** People were performing laws for God to bless and to provide for them. Jesus fulfilled the laws by dying on the cross at Calvary. This is my opinion; the laws are still needed for people who have unbelief in God and Jesus and refuse the gospel of grace message. They need to know God's character and have knowledge of Jesus's life and death; how he had sacrificed his life for sins in this world.

Clearly, God loves you unconditionally. His love for you has nothing to do with money to receive his blessing. Religion should stop sending believers in Jesus Christ on a guilt trip about tithing and offering. It may cause someone not to seek God because of money.

Tithing was in the bloodline of the traditions, priesthoods, laws of the land, and the Mosaic laws to give 10% of your income. This was done out of respect to God, and to let him know you're in a relationship with your money.

Whenever you are in any relationship, you will be offering money, your time, or something. God's law is love, you are under the gospel of grace, and faith in Jesus canceled out your works. You should want to contribute money, for the kingdom of God today out of respect to God. The truth about giving money to support the churches, God's kingdom, and his words, trust in this statement, you will receive a hundred percent back in this lifetime and in heaven.

Would a man rob God? God was telling his people to return to his covenant. God's people were under the Mosaic Laws, the Ten Commandments. The people just came out of captivity, because of their disobedience, they didn't want to follow God's laws anymore. The people were living life like they didn't need God to support them. Four hundred silent years God stopped speaking directly to his people, he was preparing the world for Jesus's coming. This is the New Testaments in the Bible. The death of Jesus was the last sacrifice to inherit heaven. God loves you through his son Jesus; therefore, his blessing will come from love, having faith in Jesus's birth, death, and resurrection. Jesus's actions cost you to lose your life to God. This is why your life doesn't belong to you if you are a child of God.

If you gain wealth in this world and lose your soul, what is your soul worth? You are under the covenant of God's gospel of grace; his grace and mercy have nothing to do with exchanging money. The message of grace is that God loves you unconditionally.

Owe no one nothing but love; loving everyone is the fulfillment of God's laws. Do not put God and money on the same level. God's character is love. Money is a tool to buy material things only on earth. You should want to be involved within all levels of life with your finances to support God's words throughout this world. God's words have made a way out of no way. **(Isaiah 55:1-2)" Ho, every one that thirsteth, come ye to the waters, and he that hath no money; come ye, buy, and eat; yea, come, buy wine and milk without money and without price. Wherefore do ye spend money for *that which is* not bread?**

and your labour for *that which* satisfieth not? hearken diligently unto me, and eat ye *that which is* good, and let your soul delight itself in fatness." The greatest investment in your lifetime on earth should be contributing money to the churches, and volunteering your time, to increase God's words around the world. **(Matthew 6:21) "For where your treasure is, there will your heart be also."** What you spend your money and time on, there is where your pleasure and heart will be.

Chapter Seven

TONGUE

In the beginning was the word, and the word was with God, he spoke and made heaven. This world existed by God and his words. **(Psalms 33:6, 9) "By the word of the LORD were the heavens made; and all the host of them by the breath of his mouth. For he spake, and it was done; he commanded, and it stood fast."** Your tongue was meant to create more than to communicate. You must use your tongue to minister the gospel of grace into this world and meditate on God's word for your blessing in life. Blessings and curses will come from your tongue. Let no corrupt communication proceed out of your mouth. **(Matthew 12:32) "And whosoever speaketh a word against the Son of man, it shall be forgiven him: but whosoever speaketh against the Holy Ghost, it shall not be forgiven him, neither in this world, neither in the *world* to come."** Evil words coming out of your mouth will defile the whole body, the nature of the tongue can send you straight to hell. **(Proverbs 18:21) "Death and life are in the power of the tongue: and they that love it shall eat the fruit thereof."**

When there is destruction in your life, it's because somewhere someone used their tongue to attack you. The tongue no one can tame; it can be deadly, and disruptive, full of poisoning statements. **(James 1:19) "Wherefore, my beloved brethren, let every man be swift to hear, slow to speak, slow to wrath:"** Watch what you say in a crisis, wicked words will pour out of your mouth; listen first, be slow to speak, and forgive everyone. Allow God's words to flow instead of your own words. Feed your soul (the heart) with God's words and let the Holy Spirit speak for you. If you safeguard your lips, you will protect your life.

Do not replay evil for evil or insult for insult, use kind words; actions of love will turn away anger and arguments. **(Matthew 12:36) "But I say unto you, That every idle word that men shall speak, they shall give account thereof in the day of judgment."** Words of wisdom full of the gospel of grace and mercy will have a greater impact on life's tragedies. Keep your tongue from evil and speaking lies; this is an honorable way to communicate. A deceitful tongue will lead you to being dishonest, distressed, a failure, and cause confusion.

Ask God to restore broken relationships, gain relief from all guilt, shame and pain by confessing your sins with repentance. Be not ashamed of the gospel of grace Jesus Christ proclaimed to this world. Spread the good news, the gossip of God's mercy, and his unconditional love he gave you through his son Jesus's death. Tell the world their sins have been forgiven with repentance and have faith in Jesus. Jesus came into the world not to condemn the world but to save the world from hell. In the beginning was a word, and the word was spoken by God. He said let there be light in this world, he spoke and transformed this entire world by his words.

Your mouth can create miracles; you have to speak to all destructions in your path. I personally think death has to obey your tongue. Do not agree to any circumstance that doesn't line up with the words of God. If you get a doctor's report of any illness, quickly speak only God's words. You were given the opportunity to escape spiritual sickness and death through the death of Jesus Christ. **(Isaiah 53:5) "But he was wounded for our transgressions, he was bruised for our iniquities: the chastisement of our peace was upon him; and with his stripes we are healed."** You have the Holy Spirit living inside your spirit. Jesus's death paid for your healing and deliverance.

You can perform miracles with your mouth when you receive the Holy Ghost Spirit, there are nine different spiritual gifts. Ask God for you to behold all nine gifts

1. Prophecy

2. Different kinds of Speaking in Tongues

3. Interpretation of Tongues, these are the gifts of Vocal Gifts

4. The Words of Knowledge

5. Words of Wisdom

6. Discerning of Spirit, these are the gifts of Revelation Gifts

7. Faith

8. Healing Hands

9. Working of Miracles.

These are the gifts of power. All gifts of the Holy Ghost Spirit come from God. **(1st Corinthians 12: 4, 6, 8-10) "Now there are diversities of gifts, but the same Spirit. And there are diversities of operations, but it is the same God which worketh all in all. For to one is given by the Spirit the word of wisdom; to another the word of knowledge by the same Spirit; To another faith by the same Spirit; to another the gifts of healing by the same Spirit; To another the working of miracles; to another prophecy; to another discerning of spirits; to another divers kinds of tongues; to another the interpretation of tongues."**

The supernatural power of the Holy Ghost Spirit will give you the power to cast out the devil and his demonic demons, healing the sick, perform miracles in Jesus's name, unexplained knowledge and wisdom, having good judgment, interpretation of dreams, speaking to God in an unknown language. Speaking in tongues is one of the nine gifts from the Holy Ghost Spirit, where you are speaking directly to God in an unknown language; therefore, the devil doesn't know what you are saying to God. You have to release the Holy Ghost Spirit to retrieve the supernatural life. Jesus gave you power of authority to speak his name, and you need to release his power in your atmosphere. You have to cast down the devil's plans with your mouth. You are in charge of sending angels or demons into your life with the words that come out of your mouth.

Your enemies will not defeat you in battle or conflicts. **(Isaiah 54:17) "No weapon that is formed against thee shall prosper; and every tongue *that* shall rise against thee in judgment thou shalt condemn. This *is* the heritage of the servants of the LORD, and their righteousness *is* of me, saith the LORD."** God's words will protect you when you are worshipping and praising him. God is a spirit and Jesus was God in a human body with the supernatural Holy Ghost Spirit controlling him. **(Number 23:19) "God *is* not a man, that he should lie; neither the son of man, that he should repent: hath he said, and shall he not do *it*? Or hath he spoken, and shall he not make it good?"** Jesus spoke the truth on how to love, and he told you to love your neighbors as yourself. Jesus has prepared a way into heaven and for you to escape hell.

Chapter Eight

PRAYING

Jesus prayed for Peter, because Satan wanted him to be the one to betray Jesus, but Jesus rebuke Satan's wish to have Simon (Peter). **(Luke 22:31-32) "And the Lord said, Simon, Simon, behold, Satan hath desired *to have* you, that he may sift *you* as wheat: But I have prayed for thee, that thy faith fail not: and when thou art converted, strengthen thy brethren."** Pray always in the name of Jesus; there is only one God and one mediator between God and you, and his name is Jesus. Jesus is at the right hand of God in heaven, speaking directly to God on your behalf. Jesus is the truth and light; the only way to God is going through Jesus. Ask and it shall be given; seek, and you will find, knock, and the door will open unto you. Pray to God in Jesus's name and watch how God will glorify his son's name in public.

Whatever you pray, believe that you will receive everything in Jesus's name. Be fearless when you are asking God for your dreams and desires. **(Hebrew 4:16) "Let us therefore come boldly unto the throne of grace, that we may obtain mercy, and find grace to help in time of need."** When you pray, ask for extravagant things for he is a gigantic God; do not put limitation on God. Do not be anxious for anything; he feeds the birds, and waters the grass, surely he will feed you. God will show up and show out on your behalf. Speak to God daily, put him on speed dial, so you can get your prayers answered quickly.

When you pray it should come from your heart. God looks on the heart. Praying will help you relax your mind when you are facing a crisis or tragedy in your life. **(Philippians 4:6) "Be careful for nothing; but in everything by prayer and supplication with thanksgiving let your requests be made known unto God."**

Pray for God to solve your problems, you should pray with repentance for your sins daily in Jesus's name. Pray for everyone that has a disease, an illness, is in pain, confused, lonely, legally in trouble, or in debt, and ask to be forgiven for all of your transgressions. You will need the Holy Ghost Spirit dwelling inside you to accomplish handling your negative feeling.

Praying will help you stay connected to God, allowing him full access in planning your life. Be confident that your prayers will be answered. Be watchful and pray that you do not enter into temptation; the spirit indeed is willing but your flesh (your soul) is weak. Praying is asking God to supply your needs, and fasting is denying your soul (the heart) and body to hear from the spirit of God. Pray this prayer when there is trouble on both sides. **(Psalms 23:1-6) "The lord is my shepherd; I shall not want. He make me laid down on green pastures; he leaded me** beside still waters. He restore my soul: he leaded me in a path of righteousness for his name sake. Yeah, though I walk through the valley of shallow of death, I will fear no evil: for thou art with me; thy rod and thy staff they comfort me. He prepared a table before me in the presence of my enemies: he anointed my head with oil; my cup running over. Surely goodness and mercy shall follow me all of the days in my life: and I will dwell in the house of the LORD for ever." It's important that you stay in love, do not allow hate or any unforgiving feelings against anyone.

Devote yourself to praying daily, be patient and faithful when you are asking God for your healing and deliverance. Pray in secret so God can reward you openly in public. Praying will make you closer to God and allow him to respond to your prayer. Also, accepted his answer to let go of everything that might be holding you hostage.

When you pray, do not have any doubt in your heart and you will receive what you prayed for. Whenever there is doubt, you are in unbelief, and whatever you are praying for might take longer to receive. God operates in faith; it is the currency of his kingdom. Praying helps you talk to God privately, you can tell him your problems in secret. If you are living a sinful life and refuse to accept the blood of Jesus and the gospel of grace, you might not want to pray to God.

Pray to remove all sinful actions in your life. Come to God in prayer with a clean heart. Understanding your rights that Jesus gave you to talk and to walk with God, no matter how you are living your life and what is happening in your life.

The best time to pray is throughout the day, especially in the morning before you start your day, and at night.

(Matthew 6:9-13) "After this manner therefore pray ye: OUR FATHER WHICH ART IN HEAVEN, HALLOWED BE THY NAME. THE KINGDOM COME. THY WILL BE DONE IN EARTH, AS IT IS IN HEAVEN. GIVE US THIS DAY OUR DAILY BREAD. AND FORGIVE US OUR DEBTS, AS WE FORGIVE OUR DEBTORS. AND LEAD US NOT INTO TEMPTATION BUT DELIVER US FROM EVIL: FOR THINE IS THE KINGDOM, AND POWER, AND THE GLORY, FOREVER AMEN." This is the most important prayer to say. You are asking God to protect your body, soul, and spirit.

Always pray for people to labor and find God's assignments for their life. Pray that you labor for God and not this world. **(Matthew 9:37-38) "Then saith he unto his disciples, the harvest truly is plenteous, but the labourers are few. Pray ye** therefore the Lord of the harvest, that he will send forth labourers into his harvest." Ask God for the assignments he prepared for your life while you are on this earth.

Jesus asked God for another alternative; he did not want to go through the pain and suffering of dying on the cross at Calvary. **(Luke 22:41-42, 44) "And he was withdrawn from them about a stone's cast, and kneeled down, and prayed, Saying, Father, if thou be willing, remove this cup from me: nevertheless not my will, but thine, be done. And being in an agony he prayed more earnestly: and his sweat was as it were great drops of blood falling down to the ground."** Jesus laid down his life for this world he died so you can live for eternity. Pray to God so he can prepare you to escape the end time, the rapture of Jesus Christ, when he comes to make heaven on earth.

Chapter Nine

FAITH

Look for Jesus, the author and the finisher of your faith. Faith is the substance of things hoped for, evidence of things not seen. God's currency is faith like money is this world's currency. It is unattainable to receive something from God without faith. Have faith in God that he will supply your needs when you ask him. **(Hebrew 11:6) "But without faith it is impossible to please him: for he that cometh to God must believe that he is, and that he is a rewarder of them that diligently seek him."** Abraham, who was the father of faith, he had faith in God to give him a child, and Sarah had a child in their old age. When their son Isaac was born, Abraham was 100 years old. Fight the good fight of faith. Lay hold on enteral life through the death of Jesus.

You should only boast about how much you love God, Jesus, and others. **(Ephesians 2:8-9) "For by grace are ye saved through faith; and that not of yourselves: it is the gift of God: Not of works, lest any man should boast.** Never talk about how good you are, because there is only one that was good enough to cancel out the world's sins and give you a place inside heaven, and his name is Jesus. Only boast about how Jesus saved you from eternal life in hell. If you believe in Jesus's death and resurrection, even those that are sleeping (dead) and in the grave he will awake when he returns to earth to make heaven on earth.

(Roman 10:17) "So then faith *cometh* by hearing, and hearing by the word of God." You should only be listening to God's words in this world. Do not look at things that you see, because those things you see are temporary, look at things that are not seen, for those things are eternal like heaven that is coming on earth. Everything in this world is subject to change, God's words will remain the same. Do not meditate or speak negative about your life, this will decrease your faith, and send demons into your life.

God only speaks to your spirit not to your flesh, listen to your spirit, this is where you will get the best ideas for your life. If you are doubting God's words, you are subject to what is happening in your life and possibly lose your miracles. Have faith in Jesus, he has cleansed you from all transgressions in your lifetime. We all have sinned, and can short of God's character. If you claim you have never sinned, most likely you are lying and the truth is not in you. **(1st John 1:9-10) "If we confess our sins, he is faithful and just to forgive us our sins, and to cleanse us from all unrighteousness. If we say that we have not sinned, we make him a liar, and his word is not in us."** When trials and tribulations come, God will not have you terrified above your capacity, he will rescue you from whatever is terrorizing you; have faith in God who has made a way for you to overcome all tragedy in your life. **(1st Corinthians 10:13) "There hath no temptation taken you but such as is common to man: but God is faithful, who will not suffer you to be tempted above that ye are able; but will with the temptation also make a way to escape, that ye may be able to bear it."** Have faith in God more than the devil; you have the knowledge of God's words, and the Holy Spirit living inside of you to kick the devil out every time he steps into your life.

A woman had issues with losing blood for twelve years. She had lost all of her money, went to several physicians, and didn't get healed. She has faith in touching Jesus's garment only to be healed. She touched his garment, He stated to her daughter, "Your faith in me has healed you". When you consider your problems more than God's words you are walking in unbelief. **(Matthew 17:20) "And Jesus said unto them, Because of your unbelief: for verily I say unto you, If ye have faith as a grain of mustard seed, ye shall say unto this mountain, Remove hence to yonder place; and it shall remove; and nothing shall be impossible unto you."** Your faith is a seed to remove all obstacle in your life. With faith nothing is insupportable for God, for those who love him, and know the words of God, he will lift you up for you are his workmanship.

Boldly speak God's word over your life having the breastplate of righteousness of Jesus's authority he gave you to use against Satan (the devil) and his demons. There will be different seasons in life on earth. **(Ecclesiastes 3:1-8) "To every*thing there is* a season, and a time to every purpose under the heaven**: **A time to be born and to die; a time to plant, and to pluck up that which is planted; A time to kill, and time to heal; a time to break down, and to build up; A time to weep, and to laugh; a time to mourn, and to dance; A time to cast away stones, and to gather stones together; a time to embrace, and to refrain from embracing; A time to get, and a time to lose; a time to keep, and to cast away; A time to rend, and to sew; a time to keep silence, and to speak; A time to love, and a time hate; a time of war, and a time of peace."** All of these things you might have to encounter in your lifetime in this world.

Have faith in Jesus who reconciled you back to God; therefore, only have faith in God's words. Do not rely on the discernment of people or this world. **(1ˢᵗ Corinthians 2:5) "That your faith should not stand in the wisdom of men, but in the power of God."** Always call on God to guide you through all life's decisions. Have faith in God, believe and you will receive.

Peter was walking on water to Jesus, when he noticed he was walking on water, he lost his faith and started to believe on his level. Peter's unbelief caused him to begin to drown. Jesus stretched out his hands and asked Peter why his faith was weak. **(2nd Corinthians 5:7) "Walk by faith not by sight."** Do not go on what you see or feel, only believe in God's words over your entire life. Have faith that God sent Jesus into this world to save your spirit from hell.

The promise through the inheritance of Abraham was not the laws, but by faith in Jesus. **(Roman 4:13-14) "For the promise, that he should be the heir of the world, was not to Abraham, or to his seed, through the law, but through the righteousness of faith. For if they which are of the law *be* heirs, faith is made void, and the promise made of none effect:"** The laws work in rage: if there were no laws, then there would be no transgression.

Cast not your confidence in faith, for it has great reward. **(Roman 14:23) "And he that doubteth is damned if he eat, because *he eateth* not of faith: for whatsoever *is* not of faith is sin."** Doubting your faith will cause the devil to attack you more, walking in unbelief is denying God's words. **(James 2:17, 26) "Even so faith, if it hath not works, is dead, being alone. For as the body without the spirit is dead, so faith without works is dead also."** Your work is having faith believing in God's promises over your problems. Have faith in Jesus's authority he gave you to heal the sick, raise the dead, cast out the devil and his demons; this is your inheritance. God did not give you the spirit of fear, only his power of love, and sound mind. Faith is more precious than money, silver, and gold; it is the currency of God's kingdom.

Chapter Ten

FORGIVING

If you are overtaken in disagreements, fight for reconciliation in every situation in life, ask God for his opinion, and never use your own solutions to solve a problem, seek God's advice first. It's vital that you come to an agreement quickly leaving no air for unforgiving in your conscience; do not be tempted to hate. Love and respect are the keys to all relationships. If you have been offended, quickly forgive as God forgave you of your transgressions. Forgiving should have no boundaries, never forgive on your level, you will need the Holy Ghost Spirit from God to forgive unconditionally. **(Galatians 6:1-2) "Brethren, if a man be overtaken in a fault, ye which are spiritual, restore such a one in the spirit of meekness; considering thyself, lest thou also be tempted. Bear ye one another's burdens, and so fulfil the law of Christ."**

Where there is unhappiness you will see emotions of hate. Don't use your own feelings to create sadness in your life. Stop feeling sadness, it is the work of the devil. Listen to the Holy Spirit to answer before you respond to any crisis in your life, hold on to forgiveness instead of pain, you will gain over everything. Do not let a day pass without forgiving everyone's transgressions against you, don't give the devil any place in your thoughts. Take the approach to forgiving everyone's transgressions without judging a problem in your natural mind. You have to give God the steering wheel to your problems quickly. **(Ephesians 4:26-27) "Be ye angry, and sin not: let not the sun go down upon your wrath. Neither give place to the devil."** You will gain good ground to solve any crisis when you make a decision to forgive every time.

If you have betrayed or hurt others, ask for forgiveness, then forgive yourself; time will heal old wounds. There is no way around not hurting someone's feelings when you cannot feel what they are feeling after you have betrayed or hurt them. Always be willing to accept and give apologies for every negative situation; for God has forgiven you of all transgression for Jesus Christ's sake. Just saying you are sorry does go a long way, the word sorry by itself is asking for forgiveness.

If you asked for forgiveness and do not receive it right away, then pray to God, ask him to allow his grace to heal all negative situation with forgiveness. There will be a time you might have to wait on forgiving and receiving forgiveness. You will be more forgiving when it is you in need of forgiveness from God. **(Mark 11:25) "And when ye stand praying, forgive, if ye have ought against any: that your Father also which is in heaven may**

forgive you your trespasses." Make sure you forgive everyone for their sins, so that God will forgive your transgressions through the blood of Jesus. **(Ephesians 1:7) "In whom we have redemption through his blood, the forgiveness of sins, according to the riches of his grace."** Jesus sacrificed himself for the world's transgressions, he provided everyone salvation. Now it is your time to offer forgiveness to everyone who trespasses against you.

The question is how many times do you have to forgive someone who has caused transgressions in your life? **(Matthew 18-21-22) "Then came Peter to him, and said, Lord, how oft shall my brother sin against me, and I forgive him? till seven times? Jesus saith unto him, I say not unto thee, until seven times: but, until seventy times seven."** You must forgive everyone's transgressions four hundred and ninety times per day. When you loved your neighbor after they betrayed and mistreated you, had someone close to you unlawfully killed or justified murdered, seek to forgive quickly because God has forgiven you for all of your sins.

Don't allow your emotions to get involve with any negative thoughts. Your emotions can take you on a roller-coast ride of hate. Hate is a horrible thought in your mind, do not allow the devil to take control over your emotions.

Mentally forgiving someone that hurt you will require your actions to be in the name of love. You must forgive everyone without questioning who's wrong or right when a crisis enters into your life. When you forgive, love is on your mind, you cannot forgive without feeling loved by God.

This is why love is the most important feeling in the world. Love will always weigh heavier in the heart than hate, if you know how God loves you. Hate is light and fast without no thoughts for compassion or understanding with no consideration that God forgave you for all transgressions.

No matter what your circumstance is, always be willing to forgive everyone at all times. Remember that Jesus died for all the unjust things that can happen to you, his blood paid the price for everyone's sins against you. Jesus was innocent, yet he took the world's punishment for sins and transgressions. Ask God to guide your life, be submissive with praying and seeking his lifestyle. Return to loving everyone and you will have a place in heaven.

(2nd Chronicles 7:14) "If my people, which are called by my name, shall humble themselves, and pray, and seek my face, and turn from their wicked ways; then will I hear from heaven, and will forgive their sin, and will heal their land."

Thank you God, for sending Jesus, he had to die for the world's sins, his death gave you immortality, and all who believe in him will escape the punishment of eternal life in hell. God has forgiven you for all of your sins; he has poured his wrath on the body of Jesus, who died in your place. Jesus was at the cross dying, he asked God to exonerate the people who was nailing him to the cross. **(Luke 23:33-34) "And when they were come to the place, which is called Calvary, there they crucified him, and the malefactors, one on the right hand, and the other on the left. Then said Jesus, Father, forgive them; for they know not what they do. And they parted his raiment, and cast lots."** Always be willing to forgive everyone at all times. You showing up with the attitude of forgiving everyone every day will reassure you are walking in love at all time. Forgiving everyone is the key to love and love is the door into heaven. Make up your mind, do you want to go to heaven or hell?

THE END

Conclusion

This book is written from the instructions of The Holy Ghost Spirit. The spirit of God put this message in my heart to release this book to you. God told me to tell you the truth about the gospel of grace message, how he loves you unconditionally, and to prepare you for Jesus's return. God wanted you to know this world belonged to you from the beginning of time; the most important thing to remember is God loves you, and love has always been the key into heaven. This book is a warning of the world antichrist systems, laws and end times, you have to choose between heaven and hell.

God's people are being destroyed; because of the lack of knowledge about the true gospel of grace message. Jesus died for you, he wanted you to know how God loves you despite the sins that you are committing in this world. It is your own faith in Jesus that will save you from hell. The gospel of grace was not given so you can continue to sin; it was giving because of God's love for you, and this world couldn't live up to God's standards.

Jesus's death purchased you from the devil, who had you under eternal condemnation. Your life does not belong to you when you have confessed Jesus is your savior; therefore, you shouldn't be making decisions without seeking God's character. The world has lost the way again becoming lovers of self. We are living in sorrowful times right now, and the end is coming. **(Luke 21:36) "Watch ye therefore, and pray always, that ye may be accounted worthy to escape all these things that shall come to pass, and to stand before the Son of man."**

Finding God's plans, gifts, and his purpose for your life before Jesus's return to this world. Jesus is coming back to make heaven on earth, he will be looking for his people, not a building, but a body that possesses his soul, spirit, and God's words in their lives. Jesus left the keys to his kingdom, start using your power of authority to cast out the devil's plans he has for your life. Start preparing for Jesus's return, he will come quickly, like a thief in the night. **(Matthew 24:36-37, 44) "But of that day and hour knoweth no *man*, no, not the angels of heaven, but my Father only. But as the days of Noah *were*, so shall also the coming of the Son of man be. Therefore be ye also ready: for in such an hour as ye think not the Son of man cometh."** Do not get caught serving yourself, this world or the devil like the days when Noah was building the Ark. Jesus is coming, be watchful, keep his spirit in your soul (the heart).